# CHILDREN and ADOLESCENTS with MENTAL ILLNESS

###### ❧

## A Parents Guide
### Edited by Evelyn McElroy, Ph.D.

WOODBINE HOUSE     1988

Copyright © 1987 Evelyn McElroy, Ph.D.
All rights reserved under International and Pan-American Copyright Conventions. Published in the United States of America by Woodbine House, Inc.

Library of Congress Catalogue Card Number: 87-051318

ISBN: 0-933149-10-7

Cover Design & Illustration: Gary A. Mohrmann
Book Design & Typesetting: Wordscape, Inc., Washington, D.C.

Library of Congress Cataloging-in-Publication Data
Children and adolescents with mental illness.
  Bibliography: p.
  Includes index.
  1. Mentally ill children. 2. Child psychiatry – Popular works. 3. Adolescent psychiatry – Popular works. I. McElroy, Evelyn M.
RJ499.C4888          1988          618.92'89          87-33989
ISBN 0-933149-10-7 (pbk.)

Manufactured in the United States of America

1 2 3 4 5 6 7 8 9 10

This book is dedicated to:

Henry Harbin, M.D. who stands out as an agent for positive change among professionals and families alike. As a psychiatrist he modified his position on ways to involve parents in family therapy and adopted encouraging and helpful educational approaches. Dr. Harbin dared to meet the challenges of the time and to continue to grow, to learn, and to change. He is an excellent professional role model.

Robert Lessey, M.D. and Jean Powell, R.N. who exemplify the best in mental health professionals. They have kept up with the current scientific approaches in their field and applied them in caring and sensitive ways.

Marcia Burgdorf, J.D., who has been a very responsive legal advocate for parents, taking time from a busy schedule to help our daughter.

The parents of the Alliance of the Mentally Ill of Baltimore.

# Acknowledgements

I wish to thank Beth Stroul for allowing Carol Howe to use material on the community support system that originally appeared in the publication, *Models of Community Support Services: Approaches to Helping Persons with Long Term Mental Illness* (1986). Stroul's report was published by the Sargent College of Allied Health Professions at Boston University.

Agnes Hatfield, Ph.D. willingly allowed some of the material that appeared in the NAMI sponsored publication, *Consumer Guide to Mental Health Services*, to be used in this book.

I wish to thank the American Psychiatric Association for allowing some of the diagnostic classifications which appear in the *Diagnostic and Statistical Manual: Third Edition, Revised*, to be reproduced in this book.

Barker Bausell, Ph.D., of the University of Maryland at Baltimore, originally developed the *Health Status Checklist*. It was modified for use with youngsters who have psychiatric problems and appears in this book in its modified form in Appendix F.

My thanks go to Robert Wardwell of HCFA who reviewed the Medicaid waiver section of this manuscript.

Thanks go to Beth Smith, of the Alliance for the Mentally Ill of North Carolina, for allowing her poem, "A Silent Cry," to be included as a parent comment.

A very warm thanks goes to my colleagues in the Department of Psychiatry at the University of Maryland, who have volunteered their time, expertise, and sensitivity to help families learn and cope with the serious mental illnesses affecting their sons and daughters. Among them are Dr. John Talbott, Dr. Russell Monroe, Dr. Eugene Brody, Dr. Anthony Lehman, Dr. Will Carpenter, Dr. Douglas Henrichs, and Dr. Paul McClelland. A special thanks goes to Dr. David Camenga, of the Neurology Department, for his understanding and help. Dr. Frieda Holt, in the School of Nursing, stands out as a person with interest in families who has offered considerable encouragement over the years.

It has been my good fortune to have as a colleague and good friend, Dr. Agnes Hatfield. I consider her writings to be among the best in terms of articulating the position of families with relatives who have mental illness. Her willingness to listen to my "positions" on various issues related to working with families has been essential in my development as a professional. This kind of critical analysis of papers, and thinking on such issues has also been performed by another good friend, Marie Killilea, in the Department of Psychiatry at Johns Hopkins University, an expert on social support systems who practices what she teaches. Finally, key members of the Curriculum and Training Task Force at NAMI created the psychological climate to reconsider helpful ways to respond to the needs of such families. These people were: Ken Terkelsen, M.D., Harriet Lefley, Ph.D., Dale Johnson, Ph.D., Kayla Bernheim, Ph.D., Claire Francell, and Vickie Conn, R.N.

Many of the families of the seriously mentally ill volunteered their own slices of life that appear as Parents Statements at the end of the chapters. The names, places, and other slight modifications have been made to provide anonymity to these individuals. Most of these people were members of the Alliance for the Mentally Ill network.

# TABLE OF CONTENTS

# Foreword

## AGNES HATFIELD, PH.D.

Several million families across the country daily face the bewilderment, frustration, and pain of having a child with a serious mental illness. It is a lonely struggle for these beleaguered families, for society generally has not been too supportive. The seriousness of these problems has been too easily dismissed as the "growing pains" of childhood or parental mismanagement of a child's behavior. But parents usually know intuitively when there is something terribly wrong with their child—even though they might have difficulty articulating what it is. Then begins a search for answers, an odyssey that may take families to an endless array of clinics, schools, and social agencies. In the recent past, it may have taken years to get any kind of satisfaction as to what was going on with their child and what to do about it.

There is reason to believe that things are beginning to change and this book is one important piece of evidence that this is so. The contributors to this book, several of whom are themselves parents of mentally ill children, provide the most essential technical knowledge needed by these families plus the "nuts and bolts" of daily management and making sound plans for the long run. Above all, a powerful message comes through in this book: Parents have the fortitude to face courageously the tragedy of their child's illness; parents are able and willing to become experts on their ill child; and they can become competent allies with professionals in the treatment of their child.

Agnes B. Hatfield, Ph.D.

---

*Agnes Hatfield, Ph.D is internationally known as a lecturer and author of several books on mental illness, including Coping With Mental Illness In the Family: A Family Guide.*

# Introduction

## EVELYN McELROY

Nothing causes parents more grief and anguish than a child or teenager afflicted with a severe psychiatric disorder. Part of the anguish comes from feeling helpless in the face of their child's psychological pain. There is no need to feel helpless. There are many ways you can make things better for your child and see that he gets the treatment he needs.

More than three million American children are thought to be suffering just as your child is suffering. These youngsters are often unable to interact well with friends, family, and other community members. Many of them do not see the world as it is most of the time. These children may have a wide variety of conditions referred to as autism, schizophrenia, mood disorders, or mental retardation coupled with mental illness or another type of severe emotional disorder.

My family has faced the crisis you are facing and we offer you our story in the hope that you will find comfort and guidance from knowing that you are not alone.

In 1981 one of our teenage daughters suddenly began exhibiting behavior indicative of a severe mental disturbance or a bad drug trip. Drug abuse was eliminated as a possible cause and we were faced with a catastrophic mental illness. Our daughter's actions, what she told us of her feelings, and how she viewed the world were unlike her normal way of responding to life. This all happened within a twenty-four hour period. One day she was a popular, bright girl who did well in school, got along as well as any other teenager with her family, and was active in her community. The next day she was in need of emergency psychiatric treatment.

As parents, we had not experienced mental illness in our families and were bewildered about the steps to take to get her the care she needed. We didn't have long to think about that since her symptoms increased in number and urgency during the next twelve hours. We had to do something fast. We rallied to the tasks facing us and did our best.

What we were most unprepared for was the way the mental health professionals viewed us. Most of them considered us to be what Maryellen Walsh termed "psychovermin." We first learned of this attitude forty-eight hours after our daughter was hospitalized when one of the nurses told us to leave the unit after I pointed out that our daughter was having a severe drug reaction. Her eyes were pulled toward her forehead and her neck was extended. We rushed to get help from the nurse and she accused us of having caused it. "She always gets worse when her family visits," she said.

At another private psychiatric hospital we were not allowed to visit our daughter. The presents we wanted to give her for her eighteenth birthday were refused by the staff. The team hung up the telephone when we called the nurses' station to ask about our daughter and were rude to us in many other ways. However, we devised a way to learn how our daughter was faring. In addition to our lawyer, our daughter's aunt and grandmother in Colorado were allowed to talk to her on the phone. Then they would call and tell us about her. During this period of time our child was not allowed to make phone calls or to have visitors, although we lived near the hospital. Such inhumane practices left deep and lasting negative feelings toward those professionals as it unnecessarily added to our distress. Our daughter later told us that she was sure that something awful had happened to all of us. Otherwise, we would be visiting and helping her with the problems she faced, as we had done for the last seventeen years.

The social worker at that hospital was *supposed* to be our link with the rest of the treatment team. She was the team spokeswoman. It was up to her to get us involved in family therapy and to function as our advocate. However, she used her role to inform my husband that I wanted to keep my daughter ill rather than let her progress in life. She had only met me a few times when she announced this verdict, which she included in her written evaluation. Despite the fact that the causes for the major mental illnesses are not fully known, this social worker had determined that the cause of our child's illness was a faulty mother-infant relationship during the first eighteen months of life. The social worker's report suffered from a lack of reliable observations and failed to consider the many successful activities my daughter and family had completed during our years together.

We also had problems with other team members. I felt a physician with a solid knowledge of psychopharmacology should be directing my daughter's care, but her physician did not seem well trained in drug treatment and barely spoke English so that we had difficulty communicating with him. He was not adequately supervised and failed to realize that he was overdosing my daughter with medication to the point that the reflex to control swallowing was shut off. She also developed a very frightening and potentially fatal side effect while under his care.

This team nearly destroyed our family. No one should have to go through such an ordeal. In addition to the psychological suffering, we paid dearly for our daughter's treatment at this hospital. It cost over $60,000 for six months of treatment there.

I continue to have feelings of rage at those professionals who violated our privacy by having us viewed through one-way mirrors without our knowledge, who held me responsible for a crime I had not committed, and who were not at all understanding or sympathetic during the greatest crisis of my life.

Basically, the team didn't understand how people normally react to a sudden and drastic illness. We were devastated by our daughter's sudden illness. Her new way of relating was not typical behavior in our family. We wanted to be with her to love and comfort her.

When youngsters suddenly become ill, it is natural for parents to want to be near their child to watch over and help him. Pediatricians have long recognized the distress a child feels when hospitalized and separated from his parents. They have humanized hospitals for the benefit of both children and their families. Families of children with mental illness also need to express their love and distress. They need to try to help when their children are ill and require hospitalization. Professionals who fail to understand these needs, disparaging them as "enmeshment," add an undeserved burden to the already heavy load parents carry.

We looked for another hospital and found a professional team that was the epitome of professional excellence. They welcomed our involvement and responded to us as people, not psychovermin. However this positive approach with this new team occurred 4,440 hours after the onset of our daughter's illness. Those six months and five days of negative experiences with other professionals were not easily forgotten. Before effective medication was found for our daughter, she was having episodes of severely impaired behavior monthly and they were increasing.

This new team developed an effective treatment plan that included our suggestions and emphasized that rehospitalizations were to be expected. The admissions would be brief and were not to be viewed as failures by ourselves or our daughter. Because the team believed it, so did our daughter. During a relapse, she commented that several of the nurses wanted her as a patient because she always got well and left the hospital sooner than the other patients. She interpreted these brief hospitalizations as successes and we never had trouble getting her admitted because of this preparation by the team. This team also helped build the foundation for other successes for our daughter which eventually led to college and a normal, happy life.

This book was written to help you as parents cope with the difficult reality facing you. For the present time, your youngster may not be able to take care of himself independently as he faces daily life. Right now he is peculiarly vulnerable. Only with a thorough knowledge of your child's illness and how it can be treated, will you be able to effectively help him.

Since many of the symptoms shown by your child may be associated with a variety of disorders, the diagnosis may take some time. Many psychiatric conditions are perplexing and require time to observe the individual and note his reactions. Be sure to demand thorough medical, neurological, and psychological procedures before a diagnosis is given your child. You want to ensure that no mistake is made and that your child will be treated for the disorder he actually has.

The families of children and adolescents with mental illnesses are often placed under severe financial and psychological strains. Because of the lack of adequate services for people with mental illness, many parents are forced to turn their homes into psychiatric hospitals because there is no other place for their child to go. You will need information on resources, treatment, and ways to manage your disturbed youth as well as guides to the unexpected obstacles that will crop up as you seek the best possible life for him. You should learn about the possibility of respite care and possible government entitlements. There is a whole bewildering world opening up before you.

The position taken in this book is that the mental illness affecting your son or daughter is *not* a family illness. Rather, our book makes the assumption that when a youngster has a mental disorder it affects the other family members but is not necessarily caused by them. Our book does not assume that there is something wrong with a family who has a troubled or mentally ill child. These families are coping with abnormal situations that demand excessive concentration, commitment, knowledge, and energy. That effort is most taxing. Their extraordinary efforts to manage life under these circumstances are awesome. The strength shown by such families is touching and often unappreciated by those who have not walked in their shoes.

Professionals can help ease the burdens facing families or their actions can add to them. They help set the stage for future therapeutic successes or failures. They need to see parents as adult learners who need to be educated about their youngster's illness and need practical advice on ways to manage problems arising from the illness or its treatment. My own story shows the many different ways professionals can view families.

Families have recently united to form a national network for education, support, and advocacy to combat the outmoded thinking of some professionals and the stigma that face families and their mentally ill relatives. The heart of any grass roots advocacy organization is the many committed people who band together to address the problems facing their loved ones. The enactment of Public Law 94–142, the Education of All Handicapped Children Act, is an example of an effective grass roots approach that eventually benefitted all disabled children.

Part of the royalties of this book will go to a grass roots organization called the National Alliance for the Mentally Ill (NAMI) to further their efforts to change how mental health professionals are educated. One of their major thrusts is to combat the stigma that professionals have long associated with families of the mentally ill. The addresses of NAMI and other family groups are listed in the back of this book.

In this book, we will help you understand what mental illness is, how to judge if your child's behavior is normal for his age or if he needs expert evaluation, and how to manuever through the bureaucratic maze.

Chapter 1 discusses what mental illness is, describes the psychiatric disorders affecting children, what the current accepted treatments are for these disorders, and how to select the best therapy for your child.

Chapter 2 is a guide showing you how to decide if your child needs expert evaluation, how to get emergency psychiatric treatment, and alerting you to the impact of mental illness on your family as a whole.

Chapter 3 discusses inpatient and residential psychiatric care and Chapter 4 covers some of the things to be aware of while your child is hospitalized and methods of helping your child rejoin the community.

Chapters 5 and 6 cover the legal provisions of education of the mentally ill, school related issues, and ways to get these educational entitlements.

Chapter 7 takes up the issue of youth suicide and what you, as parents, need to be aware of.

Chapter 8 outlines issues to answer when making long-term plans for your child's future.

If you become involved in your child's efforts to reach improved mental health, you will increase his chances for success. This should be reason enough to continue to learn, ask questions, seek answers, and plan for the future.

*CHILDREN AND ADOLESCENTS WITH MENTAL ILLNESS* reflects the thinking of the respective writers. The views and opinions I express in this book are my own and do not reflect the official policies or thinking of any organization with which I am associated.

## REFERENCES

Bowlby, J. *Attachment and Loss*. London: Hogarth Press, 1969.

Carpenter, W.T. "Approaches to Knowledge and Understanding of Schizophrenia." *Schizophrenia Bulletin* 13 (1987), no. 1: 1–8.

Engel, G.L. "The Clinical Application of the Biopsycosocial Model." *The American Journal of Psychiatry* 137:(1980) 535–44.

Goldstein, M.J. "Psychosocial Issues." *Schizophrenia Bulletin* 13 (1987), no. 1: 157–71.

Hansell, N. "Serving the Chronically Mentally Ill." In *The Modern Practice of Community Mental Health*, edited by J.H. Schulberg and M. Killilea, 358–71. San Francisco: Jossey-Bass, 1982.

Hatfield, A. "What Families Want of Family Therapists." In *Family Therapy in Schizophrenia*, edited by W.R. McFarlane, 41–65. New York: Guilford Press, 1983.

Knitzer, J. *Unclaimed Children*. Washington, D.C.: Children's Defense Fund, 1982.

McElroy, E. "Ethical and Legal Considerations for Interviewing Families of the Seriously Mentally Ill." Paper presented at the NAMI-NIMH Forum on Educating Mental Health Professionals to Work with Families of the Mentally Ill, Rockville, Maryland, February 27, 1985.

McElroy, E. "The Beat of a Different Drummer." In *Families of the Mentally Ill: Coping and Adaptation*, edited by A.B. Hatfield and H.P. Lefley, 225–43. New York: Guilford Press, 1987.

McHugh, P.R. and P.R. Slavney. *The Perspectives of Psychiatry*. Baltimore: Johns Hopkins University Press, 1983.

Rutter, M. *Helping Troubled Children*. New York: Plenum Press, 1975.

Spaniol, L. et al. "Families as a Resource in the Rehabilitation of the Severely Psychiatrically Disabled." In *Families of the Mentally Ill: Coping and Adaptation*, edited by A.B. Hatfield and H.P. Lefley, 167–90. New York: Guilford Press, 1987.

Strauss, J.S. et al. In *The Nature of Schizophrenia*, edited by L.C. Wynne et al, 617–30. New York: John Wiley and Sons, 1978.

Stroul, B.A. and R.M. Friedman. *A System of Care for Severely Emotionally Disturbed Children and Youth*. Washington, D.C.: Georgetown University Child Development Center, 1986.

Talbott, J.A., ed. "Unified Mental Health Systems: Utopia Unrealized." In *New Directions in Mental Health*. San Francisco: Jossey-Bass, 1983.

Terkelson, K.F. "Schizophrenia and the Family: II Adverse Effects of Family Therapy." *Family Process* (1983): 191–200.

Torrey, E.F. *Surviving Schizophrenia: A Family Manual*. New York: Harper and Row, 1983.

Tucker, G.J. and J.S. Maxmen. "'Rational' Hospital Psychiatry." *The Journal of Medicine and Philosophy* 11 (1986): 135–41.

Walsh, M.E. *Schizophrenia: Straight Talk for Families and Friends*. New York: W.W. Morrow & Co., 1985.

ONE

# Common Mental Illnesses of Childhood and Adolescence: Symptoms and Treatment

ALP KARAHASAN, M.D., PH.D.

Mental illness can be a bewildering world for anyone. The symptoms are rarely as clear-cut as a broken leg or the treatment as simple as a plaster cast. Some mental illnesses overlap in symptoms and others have a variety of treatments, not all of which work for every patient. Sometimes just getting a diagnosis of what is wrong with your child can be an exhausting procedure. There is no way I can address every child's illness directly, but in this chapter I hope to be able to give you broad outlines of what symptoms professionals look for in the common mental illnesses afflicting our youngsters and the accepted treatments for these illnesses. Just remember that the majority of the causes for such illnesses and their treatment are biological, and not due to upbringing.

Understanding your child's illness can make you a more effective member of your child's parent/professional team. You will understand what is happening to your child and what treatments are commonly used. You will be able to ask more informed questions and become a more effective advocate for your child.

# How Can I Tell If My Child Needs Psychiatric Help?

Deciding if your child is in need of psychiatric help can be a very difficult thing to do. Find out what others who know your child think. Get input from your child's teachers, your friends, and other family members. If you are still seriously concerned about your child's behavior, turn to the experts to get your child evaluated.

## *Your Child's Evaluation*

There are two key factors for you and your experts to consider when evaluating your child. The first is how well your youngster functions in his life spheres. The second is to determine if his behavior is normal for his stage of emotional, cognitive, and physical development.

### Life Spheres

The life spheres are made up of:

a. The home and family.
b. The community and neighborhood.
c. The school, peers, and learning behavior.

Children tend to show different symptoms in different life spheres. For instance, some depressed children might show those gloomy feelings only in school and not at home or in the community.

School teachers or counselors can be helpful if they notice what they consider to be abnormal behavior in your youngster and notify you of their concern. Once they have gotten in touch with you, you should find a professional who can help your child.

Once you and your professionals have determined that there is a problem in your child's life spheres, you must work out a treatment plan. An experienced child psychiatrist will generally try to get information from different people in the three areas of your child's life spheres and work with that knowledge to get a clear diagnosis and help develop a treatment plan. This involves tapping into the strength of your child's unaffected life sphere. It also might mean using the strengths in his happy family environment or having a supportive friendship network. For example, if your child is learning disabled and has poor self-esteem as a result of his lack of academic achievement, friends and family can be guided in ways to help boost his self esteem.

## Behavior

The second major factor to evaluate is deciding whether or not your child's behavior is normal. You need to pay very close attention to the fact that childhood mental disorders are difficult to diagnose and separate from behaviors that are different from most children of the same age and background but yet within a definition of "normal." For example, your child may spend a great deal of time alone. If he still has friends, does well in school, and seems happy as a member of your family, then he would probably still be considered "normal" although the fact that he spent so much time alone would make him "different but within the normal range." Since the definition of "normal" as opposed to "variation from normal development" is so difficult during the changing childhood years, you must make sure that your child's disturbance is, in fact, "real" and not just a behavior that is going to disappear within a short time.

In order to make sure that this is a true mental disorder you are dealing with, you will need a thorough diagnostic workup on your child. This involves a physical assessment, neurological assessment, a brain-wave test, if necessary, a CT scan (computerized tomography) test of the brain, as well as brain imaging-mapping, which allows the doctor to visualize how your child's brain functions.

Additionally, your child will need special education evaluations for the assessment of specific reading, math, and other disabilities as well as coordination problems. He will need to be psychologically tested for intelligence, scholastic abilities, and possibly the unconscious factors through the use of projective tests like the Rorschach and TAT. These assessments and procedures help your doctor decide if your child is suffering from a mental disorder or is merely deviating from a normal developmental pattern *but* within broad normal ranges.

## Who Should Direct My Child's Comprehensive Psychiatric Evaluation?

A comprehensive psychiatric evaluation requires the services of professionals who have special training in evaluating, diagnosing, and treating youngsters. This professional group is referred to as a *team*. Leading the team should be the *child psychiatrist*. A child psychiatrist is a physician who trains for an additional five years to become qualified in child psychiatry. In North America there are only about three thousand child psychiatrists, so they are in great demand as consultants to schools and other health systems concerned with the needs of children.

Other members of the team are the developmental psychologists who will test the age appropriateness of your child's development; pediatricians; social workers; and teachers with special education training who will look at possible learning disabilities and their remedies.

Your child's evaluation will require a full assessment of his biological (physical), psychological, and social functioning. The child psychiatrist uses the team to gather information from the assessment and draw up a management plan for your child's diagnosis and treatment. While the team is doing its evaluation, it is up to you to see that they work as a united group. If you are hearing different messages from certain members of the team, ask for clarification from the team leader—the child psychiatrist. Although your role is limited at this time, you are still a member of the team and an important one. You are the person who has overall responsibility for your child and you will need to be involved from the beginning.

# Getting The Diagnosis
## *Diagnostic and Statistical Manual*

Once the team has decided on a diagnosis, they will have something to work with in prescribing a treatment plan. Most of the terms they will use come from the *Diagnostic and Statistical Manual of Mental Disorders (Third Edition-Revised)* referred to as DSMIIIR. You will need to become familiar with this handbook yourself since it is used by all insurance companies, school systems, and professionals. It will give you definitions of the terms your team uses and includes clinical examples that may help you. The Reading List at the back of this book will tell you how to order this manual.

## *Disability*

Your team may use the term *disability*. The degree of suffering, the social restrictions, the interference with development, and the effects on others must be considered to determine if your child's psychiatric disorder is causing enough impairment to warrant using the term disability.

A mental disability basically is an emotional or physical impairment which:

A. Has emotional or behavioral symptoms.
B. Is not solely a result of other problems such as epilepsy or alcoholism.
C. Continues for more than one year *or* is likely to continue for more than a year on the basis of a specific diagnosis.
D. Results in *substantial* functional limitations of major life activities in two or more of the following areas:
   1. self-care at appropriate developmental levels;
   2. perceptive and expressive language;
   3. learning;
   4. self-direction, decision-making, judgement;
   5. capacity for living in a family setting.

We will be dealing with disabilities in this chapter, although we will mention briefly other problems that can occur alone but often occur in combination with the mental disabilities facing our youngsters. Once you have the definition of disability you must understand that the diagnosis, the length of your child's problem behavior, and his response to treatment are all assessed together to decide if he has a disability for which he needs medical help. A disability generally leads to a combination of team-planned care, treatment, and other services.

## Treatment

Your child's treatment should be planned with caution, detail, and tailored to his individual needs since no two children will have the same treatment needs. It is important that he be treated as soon as possible. As with most illnesses, mental illness responds better if treated in the early stages.

You will be working with your child's psychiatrist in a variety of ways: getting a diagnosis, planning his treatment, and getting him the services he needs in order to have his illness treated and bring him back into the family to go on with his life.

You will need to work with your child psychiatrist to represent your child when dealing with the school authorities and disability (social security) authorities. Part of the child psychiatrist's role should be advocating for your child in collaboration with you.

Sometimes there may be areas of disagreement between you and the child psychiatrist. When that happens, usually the psychiatrist will tell you his version of your child's treatment needs. As long as this conflict is handled with respect and an honest desire to get the best possible treatment for your child, there should be no serious problem. If worst comes to worst, you may need to get a second opinion to resolve your differences.

The next section of this chapter deals with the more common mental illnesses, their symptoms, and a brief outline of the usual treatments for these illnesses. Appendix A will cover the specific medications prescribed for these illnesses and the possible side effects.

# The Major Categories Of Mental Illness

Your child will probably be diagnosed as having a disability within one of four major categories of mental illness. It is a good idea to try to understand all you can about the diagnosis so when the treatment team presents its treatment plan to you, you will be able to see how each aspect of the plan relates to a part of your child's problem.

The four major categories are listed below with explanations of the factors your treatment team will take into account when diagnosing your child and an outline of general treatments. Remember, every child is an individual and his treatment will be planned for him on an individual basis.

## *Affective Disorders (Mood Disorders)*

Mood disorders are mental illnesses that affect the emotional balance of a person. There is mounting evidence that many of these mood disorders have a physical basis. Generally we separate these disorders into *Bipolar Affective Disorder* and *Major Depressions.* Recent studies have linked the causes of some types of bipolar affective disorders to defective genes. It is known that people suffering from either of these disorders have abnormal biochemical brain functions. The strong probability is that there is a genetic predisposition to this disorder that runs in families. Approximately 10 percent of the adult population suffers from a mood disorder.

### Bipolar Affective Disorder

This disorder, once known as manic/depression, is found less frequently in children than in adults, but it does occur. If your child has been diagnosed as having a bipolar affective disorder, then he suffers episodes of depression and mania (extreme elation) with periods of normal feelings in between. It is as if he were a clock pendulum with his moods swinging from ecstacy all the way on the right to deep depression all the way to the left. In the middle would be the range of normal feelings. The length of these mood swings differs from person to person as does the number of episodes.

When your child is manic, he feels able to conquer anything. There are no barriers that he can perceive, no problems to overcome. He may indulge in spending sprees, get little sleep, and speak rapidly and laugh continuously. When he is depressed, he may be unable to function at all or if he can manage to get out of bed, he moves slowly, as if he has a heavy weight on him. His grades suffer, his self-esteem is poor, and he may even be suicidal.

**Treatment.** Mood regulators, such as Lithium, and supportive psychotherapy are the treatments of choice. Medications to supplement the effects of the mood regulators are given, depending on your child's response to treatment. Your child will need to face the probability that this disorder will be a lifelong condition and is something he, and you, need to take into consideration. It might be helpful to have both a short-term, and a long-term stress management plan. There are self help groups that may prove helpful, both for you and your child. For further information on medications, see Appendix A.

## Major Depression

This disorder is more commonly known as severe or clinical depression. It is recurrent, long lasting, and life threatening. You need to know that children get depressed almost as frequently and severely as adults. Children will hide their depression more readily with hyperactivity and distraction than adults. It is fairly common for children to be treated for hyperactivity, learning disabilities, laziness, or destructive behavior while the primary problem is a clinical depression.

Youngsters with an untreated clinical depression are at risk for suicide attempts. This is such a real risk that this book has devoted an entire chapter, Chapter 7, to this problem.

In order for your child to be diagnosed as having a major depressive disorder, he must have at least five of the following symptoms for at least two weeks:

1. He is depressed or irritable most of the time.

2. His pleasure in all, or almost all, his normal activities has dropped significantly.
3. He has lost, or gained, more than 5 percent of his body weight, or has not made his expected weight gain.
4. He has insomnia or hypersomnia.
5. He is either very restless or very slowed down.
6. He is tired most of the time.
7. He has feelings of worthlessness or excessive guilt feelings.
8. He is indecisive and finds it difficult to think or concentrate.
9. He has recurrent thoughts of death.

For this diagnosis, your child must have no physical illness that started this episode or be experiencing a normal reaction to the loss of a loved one. He must not have experienced delusions or hallucinations in this two week time period and must not be suffering from another mental illness.

**Treatment.** The most common treatment is hospitalization followed by a combination of drug therapy, psychotherapy, and exercise after the patient is released. Lithium is widely used to stabilize brain function and antidepressants such as Elavil or Norpramine are prescribed for the depressive episodes. Psychotherapy is aimed at treating any emotional problems a child might have as well as helping the child learn how to manage his illness. Exercise is nature's way to help regulate moods and is an important addition to drug therapy. Usually a psychiatrist recommends twenty minutes of aerobic exercise at least three times a week. See Appendix A for a more complete listing of medications.

## Pervasive Developmental Disorders

With the pervasive developmental disorders, the brain has trouble correctly processing information. Due to the problems associated with the neurons of the central nervous system and specifically the brain, your child's perception of reality is faulty. We can expect symptoms to appear in the areas of information integration, communication, socialization, imagination, and motor skills.

According to many specialists, these developmental difficulties or delays are a category of illnesses characterized by:

1. Impairment in your child's social interaction abilities.
2. Impairment in his development of verbal and nonverbal communications.

3. Poor imagination and empathy.

These children often have the same pervasive lack of responsiveness to other people, exhibit gross deficits in language development as well as speech oddities, display bizarre responses to their environment, resist change, fail to form attachments, and are often incoherent. The degree of the developmental delay differs from one child to another as well as from one end of the spectrum of the disorder to the other.

## Autistic Disorder (Infantile Autism)

This is the most severe of the pervasive developmental disorders. In order to diagnose autism, there must be a diagnosable onset before thirty-six months of age; lack of responsiveness to others; gross language deficits, including no speech or peculiar speech patterns and delayed repetitions or metaphorical language, pronoun reversal (such as mixing up "I" and "you"); bizarre responses to situations, attachment to peculiar food objects or living objects. Any child who meets the American Psychiatric Association's criteria for this developmental disorder must have these symptoms within the first three years of life.

Symptoms of the illness are as follows:

1. A sudden excessive anxiety manifested by a catastrophic panic reaction to a normal everyday occurrence and, at the same time, an inability to be consoled when upset over these occurrences.
2. Constrictive or inappropriate emotions, including a lack of appropriate peer reactions, as well as disproportionate anger and rage reactions, and mood shifts.
3. A dislike of change in their environment (such as a change of dinner time or moving furniture).
4. Oddities of motor movement such as peculiar posturing, hand and finger movements, hand flapping, toe walking, and stomping.
5. Abnormalities of speech, such as melody-like talk, ending statements in a question-like tone, or using a monotonous voice.
6. Increased or decreased sensitivity to external stimuli such as touching, sound, or changes in body posture.
7. Self-mutilating behavior.

**Treatment.** A multi-faceted approach by a team of experts is required to address this condition. Treatment includes the following:

1. To provide highly structured, predictable surroundings in which your child might respond and adjust.
2. To have caring, competent, and compassionate adults in your child's environment to help him learn to socialize. Parents might be regarded as co-therapists.
3. To create opportunities for teaching, stimulating, and practicing all forms of human communication. Speech and language development is stressed.
4. To channel your child's special abilities and interests toward social goals. His deficiencies are considered in devising programs to motivate him to engage in and enjoy new activities.
5. Stereotyped (repetitive) movements are discouraged or incorporated into useful activities.
6. Speech therapy, perceptual-motor training, and experiences in group activities, as well as cognitive training are usually provided on a continuing and intensive basis. Often this takes place in a special day school.
7. Individual psychotherapy.
8. Drug therapy may include:
   a. the use of sedating or tranquillizing agents,

Support and education for the family on ways to understand, cope, and rehabilitate the child is essential.

If your child is over thirty-six months of age and younger than twelve years old; meets three out of the seven criteria presented above; and there are no delusions, hallucinations, or abnormal view of reality, then your child may be suffering from pervasive developmental disorder.

**Pervasive Developmental Disorder Not Otherwise Specified**

In this category, children display certain deviations in the development of basic psychological functions such as social skills, language, or motor movements. If your child only has motor deficits and isolated social skill deficits, then he would be diagnosed as having an atypical pervasive developmental disorder not otherwise specified.

**Treatment.** The treatment may consist of individual psychotherapy, group counseling, and perceptual-motor integration approaches. The treatment plan would consider your child's strengths and weaknesses and would aim to maximize his abilities. Parents as allies and co-therapists will be used on the team.

## Specific Developmental Disorders

These disorders are characterized by inadequate development of specific academic, language, speech and motor skills that are not due to other illnesses. They are listed below:

1. Developmental Arithmetic Disorder
2. Developmental Expressive Writing Disorder
3. Developmental Reading Disorder
4. Developmental Articulation Disorder
5. Developmental Expressive Language Disorder
6. Developmental Receptive Language Disorder
7. Developmental Motor Coordination Disorder

## *Disruptive Behavior Disorders*

### Attention Deficit/Hyperactivity/Learning Disabilities Disorders

It is thought that these disorders are caused by immature growth in certain areas of the brain. Sometimes the brain matures enough for the disorder to disappear without treatment. Even if this happens, these children usually have significant problems as a result of the years spent with these disorders. These disabilities have certain elements in common although each child will have these symptoms in varying degrees. These symptoms are inappropriate degrees of inattentiveness, impulsiveness, and hyperactivity. Generally the symptoms will appear at home as well as at school and at play. These children are generally quite accident prone and in motion almost constantly. They run around, fidget, and continuously handle objects.

In very young preschool children, the most prominent feature is gross motor hyperactivity, such as excessive running and climbing. In older children and teenagers, the most prominent feature is fidgeting and restlessness. This restlessness often interferes with learning and social activities.

Children's symptoms will typically worsen when they are under stress or required to apply themselves intensely, as in a learning situation. No sign of these symptoms will appear if the child is in a new or entertaining situation that captures his interest. The onset of this disorder must be before the age of seven and last at least six months. The condition must not be due to any type of schizophrenia, depression, or severe or profound mental retardation. Although children must have demonstrated the symptoms of this disorder before the age of seven, generally they will not be referred to pediatricians or psychiatrists until they are between the ages of eight and ten, usually by the school. This time lag is due to the time needed for you and your child's teachers to realize there is a problem and then judge the severity of it. As I mentioned earlier in the chapter, it is very difficult to judge what is within the range of "normal" and what isn't.

If your child is suspected of having this disorder, then see that he is evaluated according to the following guidelines:

**Attention Deficits.** At least eight of the following fourteen symptoms must be present:
1. Often fails to finish things he starts.
2. Often doesn't seem to listen.
3. Is easily distracted.
4. Has difficulty concentrating on school work or other tasks requiring sustained attention.
5. Has difficulty sticking to play activity.

**Impulsiveness.**
6. Often acts before thinking and doesn't always consider consequences of his actions (dangerous activities).
7. Shifts excessively from one activity to another.
8. Has difficulty organizing work, often loses things necessary for tasks (books, pencils, etc.).
9. Frequently calls out in class.
10. Has difficulty waiting his turn in games or group discussions, often intrudes on others.

**Hyperactivity.**
11. Has difficulty sitting still or fidgets excessively.
12. Has difficulty staying seated.
13. Often talks excessively.
14. Is always "on the go," or acts as if "driven by a motor," and has difficulty playing quietly.

**Treatment.** In general, the treatment involves the use of stimulant medications such as Ritalin (Methylphenidate) and Cylert (Magnesium Pemoline). The theory is that the poorly connected centers of the brain integrate information slowly causing faulty communications between various brain centers and leading to a generalized slowing down of perception and data integration. Supposedly, the stimulant medications correct the neural transmission. Currently, some medications classified as antidepressants, such as Norpramine, have also been effective in the treatment of hyperactivity/attention deficit disorders. Generally, both the symptoms of hyperactivity and inattentiveness respond to stimulant medication. Appendix A describes some of the medications used in the treatment of this disorder.

The most important issue for you to consider is that your child must not be allowed to succumb into a secondary depression and develop poor self-esteem due to his disorder. Many children are aware that they are somehow "different" than their peers and may feel inferior. You cannot afford to ignore his problem. You should counsel your child openly and explain the problem, the treatment, and its ramifications so that he clearly understands what is happening to him. Stress that there are ways he can learn to compensate for his disorder. It may be necessary to use psychotherapy and/or group therapy. Your child must be told over and over that he has a problem *not* that he is a problem.

During the teenage years, most children will learn to compensate for the developmental delay and have little or no further problems. Since most children "grow out" of this disorder when their brains fully mature, it is very important to make sure that no educational deficits develop while waiting for this maturation process. Your child should be tutored in the summer vacations to prevent "forgetting" and from experiencing other skill lapses. He should be encouraged to expand his knowledge through all possible means.

## Oppositional Defiant Disorder

The essential feature of this disorder is a pattern of negativistic, hostile, and defiant behavior. Your child may be given this diagnosis if he meets at least five of the following nine criteria:

1. Often loses his temper.
2. Often argues with and insults people.

3. Often defies adult rules; usually refuses adult requests.
4. Often deliberately does things that annoy other people.
5. Often blames others for his own mistakes.
6. Is often touchy or easily annoyed by others.
7. Is often angry and resentful.
8. Is often spiteful and vindictive.
9. Often swears and uses obscene language.

The severity of the oppositional defiant disorder ranges from mild to severe depending on how many of the characteristics the child displays and how great is his impairment at school and in a social setting.

**Treatment.** Psychotherapy that uses structure and predictability and is given by caring and sensitive adults is helpful. It is important to show the youngster how his behavior affects others. Establishing and setting limits is critical to the success of treatment. Teaching parents how to employ strategies that reinforce positive behavior is needed.

## The Anxiety Disorders of Childhood or Adolescence

These patterns of behavior tend to occur when the child is separated from "significant others." The younger child may create a fuss when left at school by his parent and a teenager may express his anxiety at leaving home by avoiding school. The younger child generally worries about his mother's well-being during his school hours. Therefore the so-called "school phobia" is not a fear of school but indeed a fear of being away from home and parents. The actions of the youngster will vary according to his age and circumstances. DSMIIIR classifies three types of these anxiety disorders:

1. Separation Anxiety Disorder;
2. Avoidant Disorder of Childhood or Adolescence;
3. Overanxious Disorder.

**Treatment.** The treatment generally consists of psychotherapy, concurrent parent-child therapy, and family therapy. If drug therapy is indicated, most of the antidepressant medications of the Imipramine and Amitriptyline group seem to be effective. (See Appendix A).

In older teenagers, it is advisable to use the nonaddictive group of sedatives, Buspirone (trade name Buspar). This anxiolytic medicine has been successfully used in reducing the neurotic types of phobic anxieties as most of the Benzodiazapines (e.g., Valium, Librium, etc.), but they are not addictive and work safely on the central nervous system.

## Schizophrenic Disorders

These disorders are thought to represent many different illnesses probably having a variety of causes, but not all the causes are known at this time. Approximately one third of the persons with schizophrenia never have another episode, and another third have only periodic relapses that make it possible for them to function adequately between these relapses. Another third deteriorate progressively.

### What Is Schizophrenia?

Schizophrenic disorders are basically disorders of thinking rather than mood. Such conditions are rare among children, but about 75 percent of the newly diagnosed cases of schizophrenia occur in people between the ages of sixteen and twenty-four.

### What Causes Schizophrenia?

No one knows for sure what causes schizophrenia. There are a number of differing theories. Some of these theories are:

1. **Genetic.** There is no definitive proof to this theory yet, although there is a greater proportion of persons with schizophrenia in families of others with this illness. More research is needed.
2. **Biochemical.** Research on the brain has resulted in promising leads. Brains of people with schizophrenia appear to have structural and functional differences from the norm.
3. **Nutritional.** There is no evidence that food, vitamin, or mineral deficiencies cause schizophrenia.
4. **Infectious Disease.** There is no conclusive evidence that viruses cause changes in the brain resulting in schizophrenia. More research is needed in this area.
5. **Psychoanalytic and Family Interaction.** There is no supporting data for this theory. Modern studies have come up with a great deal of evidence that parents are *not* to blame for their children's illness.
6. **Stress.** There is no evidence that this causes schizophrenia.
7. **Drug Abuse.** Obviously this can't help any illness, but there

is no evidence that it actually causes schizophrenia. However, all illicit drugs and alcohol facilitate the occurrence of the illness.

## Will My Child Get Schizophrenia If A Member of Our Family Has It?

There is a 10 percent chance that your child will get schizophrenia if one of his parents has the condition, as compared to a 1 percent chance for the general population. If both parents have schizophrenia then a child's chances go up to 39 percent. If your child's nonidentical twin has schizophrenia then his chances are about 10 to 15 percent. However, if his identical twin has the illness, then his chances increase to 35 to 50 percent have getting schizophrenia.

## How Can I Tell If My Child Has Schizophrenia?

In order for your youngster to be diagnosed as having schizophrenia, he must have the following:

A. The presence of (1), (2), or (3) for at least one week.
  (1) Two of the following:
    a. Delusions (believing things that are widely opposed to reality, such as believing he is God);
    b. Hallucinations (seeing, hearing, smelling, touching, or tasting things that are not actually there). These must occur frequently and last longer than a few moments.;
    c. Incoherence;
    d. Catatonic behavior;
    e. Flat or grossly inappropriate actions.
  (2) Bizarre delusions (for example believing that he is being controlled by a dead person, or someone is sending him thought messages).
  (3) Prominent hallucinations (for example, hearing a voice keeping a running commentary in his brain, or two voices talking to each other).

He must also have:
B. Significantly impaired functioning in his normal life spheres.
C. No other mental illnesses.
D. Signs of the disturbance for at least six months. This six-month period must include an active phase of at least one

week, less if the symptoms are being treated successfully. The active phase is generally considered to be that time when he actually believes he is God, or is actually hearing voices. He must also have psychotic symptoms with or without a prodromal or residual phase as described below.

**Prodromal Phase.** A clear deterioration in functioning before the active phase, not due to a mood disturbance or drug abuse. For instance, before he starts hearing voices, there is a period of time when he behaves strangely in other ways. He wanders around the house, gets little sleep, and seems to have difficulty remembering what he was planning to do. If he has any two of the prodromal symptoms listed below, then he is in the prodromal phase.

**Residual Phase.** Following the active phase, persistence of at least two of the symptoms listed below, not due to a mood disturbance or drug abuse.

**Prodromal or Residual Symptoms.**
1. Marked social isolation or withdrawal.
2. Marked impairment in functioning.
3. Markedly peculiar behavior.
4. Deterioration in personal hygiene and grooming.
5. Blunted or inappropriate affect.
6. Strange speech patterns.
7. Odd beliefs or magical superstitions influencing behavior.
8. Recurrent illusions.
9. Marked lack of initiative, interests, or energy.
E. No organic cause for this illness can be found.
F. If there is a history of autism, the additional diagnosis of schizophrenia can be made only if prominent delusions or hallucinations are also present.

**Treatment.** Treatment of schizophrenia today usually involves medications tailored to the individual patient. It is a good idea to have your youngster educated about his illness and his medications. Have his doctor explain these facts to him. Get books and discuss them with him. If possible, have him read them himself. Then if there are side affects, you and he can negotiate with his doctors about dosage levels and types of medications. Appendix A covers this in more detail.

In addition to medication, psychotherapy can help your youngster cope with life situations and his illness. A supportive family, and a long-term management plan are also important.

Most of the mental illnesses call for some form of therapy, either medication therapy alone or in combination with psychotherapy. The next section of this chapter describes both forms of therapy and gives you a list of things to consider when choosing a therapy method and psychotherapist.

# Types Of Therapies

There are two general types of therapies that your child with mental illness may come in contact with as his illness is being treated. There is medication therapy which focuses on changing your child's behavior by means of medications. And there is psychotherapy which focuses on changing your child's behavior by working on his emotional responses, weaknesses, and strengths.

## Medication Therapy

The treatment for many mental illnesses includes medications. If your child is prescribed any medication, be sure he is monitored by a physician who is an expert such as a general psychiatrist or a child and adolescent psychiatrist.

### How The Brain Works

In order for you to understand how medications work, you need to understand a little about how the brain itself works. The brain controls both the body and the emotions. It does this by processing and acting on information it receives. In order to process information, the brain depends on biochemical messengers, called *neurotransmitters*. These neurotransmitters transmit information from one nerve cell, or *neuron*, to another. In this way thoughts, feelings, and messages are conveyed through the transmission of these *impulses*.

One neuron is separated from the adjacent neuron by a tiny gap called a *synapse*. In order for the impulse to get from one neuron to another, it must cross the synapse. Neurotransmitters carry the impulse across. This transfer is how the neurons in our brain talk to each other. The synapses have what we call *receptor sites* to hold the neurotransmitters as they ferry the impulses.

Different neurotransmitters have different jobs. The ones we are interested in help regulate emotions. They include *dopamine, norepinephrine,* and *serotonin* neurotransmitters.

**Dopamine.** Persons with schizophrenia show an abnormally high density of receptors in the brain for dopamine. Antipsychotic medication acts in those synapses which use dopamine by binding with dopamine receptor sites and blocking the effects of the neurotransmitter dopamine. Because they work on the dopamine receptor sites, these same drugs have been found to be effective in treating a bipolar affective disorder.

**Norepinephrine.** The predominant theory on the cause of bipolar affective disorder is that the manic phase may be related to a shift in levels of certain neurotransmitters, especially norepinephrine. Norepinephrine tends to make us feel good. High levels may be found in the manic phase and decreased levels in the depressed phase of a bipolar affective disorder.

Antidepressant drugs increase norepinephrine levels. One group of drugs does this by inhibiting the action of an enzyme called *monoamine oxidase* (MAO) which is responsible for deactivating norepinephrine in the neuron. Another group of antidepressents is known as *tricyclics.* They are believed to increase norepinephrine levels by blocking removal of the norepinephrine from the synapse.

**Serotonin.** Serotonin helps regulate your body temperature, control the onset of sleep, and is involved in sensory perception. Low levels of serotonin have been linked to suicide attempts and certain types of social behavior.

## Other Drugs

There are a variety of other mood regulators and drugs to aid in the control of mental illness. One of the best known is *Lithium,* which is technically not a drug but an element. It has been effective in controlling the wide mood swings of depression and mania although so far we don't known exactly why it works as well as it does.

Other drugs may act to depress the central nervous system of which the brain is a part. Alcohol slows down the action of neurons and may depress the part of the brain that controls inhibitions. Valium appears to depress the part of the brain where emotion is settled. Other drugs, like caffeine and amphetamines, may stimulate the brain.

For reasons we don't know, amphetamine-like compounds have been successfully used to calm down hyperactive children and may also increase a person's level of concentration.

There are still a lot of questions about how the brain itself works. There are also a lot of questions about why drugs work as they do on the brain. We have a long way to go in medical research, but as we learn more about the brain, we also learn more about how medications work on the brain. Newer and more effective drugs are definitely going to be part of our children's treatment in the future.

## Psychotherapy

The other half of your child's treatment is psychotherapy. The following list of types of therapies should help you decide which is most appropriate for your child. Discuss them with your child's psychiatrist and get her recommendations. This should be a joint decision of the parent/professional team.

### Individual Therapy

This form of treatment involves regularly scheduled talks between your child and a therapist. The aim is for your child to learn more about himself by sharing thoughts and feelings with a trained, understanding, and experienced therapist. The therapist should have positive experience in treating people with a similar diagnosis. There are several different forms of individual psychotherapy. Here are a few to keep in mind when selecting a therapist for your child.

**Interpersonal Psychotherapy.** This form of therapy focuses upon problems your child has in dealing with other people. The therapist focuses on what is happening in your child's life now and looks for links between your child's mood, feelings, and important past events that may be associated with the current troubles. Your child and the therapist work together to change his behavior and social skills.

**Insight-Oriented Psychotherapy.** Insight-oriented types of therapy proceed from the assumption that patients can be helped by a better understanding of themselves. These therapies operate at several levels. Some aim to uncover unconscious impulses and to analyze long standing early memories. This process theoretically increases self-knowledge and frees up energy that your child would otherwise use to keep the unconscious impulses under control. These psychotherapies aim to treat the "whole person," not merely the symptoms. They are often referred to as psychodynamic therapies.

A crucial priority in this therapy is the *transference relationship*, where your child projects perceptions and feelings about important childhood persons onto the therapist. The therapist will interpret this behavior to your child and help him find ways to change it. This can be an extended process taking several years and requires a therapist with a supportive and caring attitude.

Insight and process-oriented therapies are most commonly chosen for patients who are at least of average intelligence and have mild personality disorders or mild to moderate psychological disturbances. They are rarely recommended for persons suffering from severe psychotic or extreme personality disorders.

**Crisis Intervention.** This therapy concentrates on getting rid of the immediate problem through behavior therapy techniques, support, reassurance, direct advice, or medication. The emphasis will often depend on the nature of the crisis and the circumstances involved.

**Supportive Therapy.** The therapist gives your child a feeling of belonging and security in their relationship. He then often feels less anxious and depressed. Once the stress of the crisis is reduced by supportive therapy, he may be able to cope with the problems that led to the psychological turmoil. The focus is on present problems and difficulties, not on past events. The therapist should have an attitude of genuine interest and concern and a desire to help. The therapist aims to reestablish your child's previous successful coping patterns. He does not attempt to provide insights although he may suggest ways for your child to cope better in the future.

**Behavior Therapy.** Behavior therapy focuses on helping your child change his inappropriate behaviors and develop and maintain more positive behaviors. This usually takes the form of direct modification of your child's life style. The therapist may examine each behavior in isolation and design an intervention strategy for it. The therapist usually begins by identifying small and specific targets of behavior to change. Gradually, as these behaviors are modified, different and more complex behavioral modification approaches are emphasized. People with phobias do well with these approaches.

**Cognitive Therapy.** Cognitive therapy is designed to help people who hold mistaken beliefs about themselves and the world around them. The aim here is to help them identify, analyze, and change these irrational beliefs. This is done by shifting perceptions from those that are unrealistic and harmful to those that are rational and useful. There is a wide range of techniques for making these perceptual shifts and they have been very useful for individuals with mild to moderate degrees of depression, and other psychological disturbances.

## Group Therapy

Group therapy focuses on learning from the experiences of others. Your child can check out his perceptions by comparing them against the perceptions of his peers. Your child has to be able to experience some pressure without undue distress for these methods to be beneficial.

## Self-Help Groups

Self-help groups are usually not led by a professional therapist, but the groups can be very helpful because the members provide mutual support and comfort to one another as the members face common problems. You can contact the Mental Health Association or the local branch of the Alliance for the Mentally Ill to learn of the types of self-help groups that might be available in the community for your child. Even if he doesn't want to go at first, gently encourage him to reach out to others. It can help him a great deal to hear other people's problems and it is one way for him to get past the stigma he may feel at having a mental illness.

## Family Therapy

Family therapy focuses on treating the family as a unit. The family members usually meet with a therapist to learn how to better understand each other's viewpoint. Family therapy can provide a way for the therapist to offer the family needed support and understanding in a time of crisis. It will help if family members are clear about what their goals are in participating in this aspect of treatment and convey that information to the therapist in advance. Often families are not fully aware of the strategies that some family therapists may use until the therapy is well underway. If you find that such treatment is increasing your distress, call a halt to it and seek other ways of getting information and support. If you can anticipate what the side effects of such therapy may be for your whole family, then you can better judge if this is something you want to get involved in. Don't decide in a hurry. *Allow at least a week to consider all the elements and side affects of such a decision.* You may wish to contact your local chapter of the Alliance for the Mentally Ill to learn how their members view family therapy approaches.

As you can see, there are a number of different types of therapies. It is a good idea to know what type of therapy you think would be best for your child. Consult with his physician and get recommendations from both professionals and parent support groups.

Once you have decided on a therapy type, then you can look for a therapist that practices that type of therapy. Here again, the same people can help you find the therapist your child needs. Be cautious about referrals that you request from professional organizations or hospitals. They are no guarantee of professional excellence. In fact, Dr. Torrey, a distinguished psychiatrist, has pointed out that physicians with impending malpractice claims are often still on referral lists. Picking a therapist certified by professional organizations usually is a good idea but still no guarantee of the quality of care the therapist will provide. You will want to have some way of evaluating the psychotherapist yourself. The following list of factors to consider should help you make your decision.

**Factors to Consider in Choosing a Psychotherapist.**
You want a therapist who does the following:
1. Recognizes that the serious mental illness affecting your child is real. She understands that many mental illnesses may be the result of biochemical abnormalities in the brain. Psychological and social consequences occur as a result of the illness. Therefore, a biological, social, and psychological treatment plan is required to treat these illnesses.
2. She conducts a thorough psychiatric, medical, and neurological examination on all her patients. She observes your child long enough to be relatively certain of her diagnosis. The results of her examination are incorporated into a treatment plan. This plan includes other medical conditions that coexist with the mental illness.
3. She works well with the other people important to your child's welfare like you, his doctor, and his family.

4. She treats both you and your child in a dignified manner.
5. She keeps up with the scientific research on mental illness.
6. She works actively for the best interests of your child wherever necessary including the hospital, educational system, insurance companies, and other professionals.
7. She is knowledgeable about medication treatment also known as "pharmacotherapy."
8. She is available to you when you need her.
9. She knows what community resources are available to help your child.
10. She is willing to share nonconfidential information about your child with you and **welcomes your input.**

## Tips on Selecting a Therapist

1. If your child requires medication, then you will want to select a psychiatrist who knows about this treatment approach. Only physicians can order medication. It is a good idea to get a recommendation from someone who has experience with a condition like your child's.
2. Fill out your Health Status Checklist in Appendix F and give it to the therapist you are considering. Ask her if she treats people with the characteristics of your youngster.
3. Find out how much she charges. If you have insurance, inform her of what your coverage is. If you are on medical assistance, ask her if she takes patients who are under the medicaid program. Some therapists don't.
4. Let her know that you are interested in helping in your child's treatment at home and that you will need advice from her as to how to best assist her.

## Other Treatments

Along with both medications and psychotherapy, there often needs to be a radical change in your child's environment. He may have to be hospitalized and the next three chapters deal more extensively with hospitalization. Although he will still need education, he might have to get his schooling in a special educational environment. Chapters 5 and 6 will go into that more fully. His treatment plan may call for him to enter either a day program or a residential treatment facility. These vary widely in availability and services offered. For more information on what is available in your area, contact your Mental Health Association or the National Alliance for the Mentally Ill.

### Day Programs

Many individual, group, family, and rehabilitation therapies are available in community mental health centers (CMHC). Day programs are also frequently offered in the CHMCs or are attached to local hospitals.

A day program is useful for children who need some kind of structure to their day to help with the transition from hospital to home. They may take the form of *psychosocial centers* with a clubhouse atmosphere. Older teenagers with severe problems in living may be candidates for such transitional programs surrounded by people who understand their strengths and weaknesses. Younger children will need a different type of day program that considers their individual learning, educational, and rehabilitation needs. These programs are known as "psychoeducational centers." The CMHCs as facilities are federal and state funded and provide treatment for persons with mental illnesses. Their fees depend on the parents' ability to pay.

### Residential Placements

Residential placements outside of the home where structure, supervision, education, and treatment are provided in a live-in treatment center is also a possibility for youngsters who for one reason or another cannot live at home. Like hospitals, these facilities vary in scope and quality. Each state has regulations concerning the licensing of them. You can use the same criteria described in Chapter 3 for selecting hospitals to find an appropriate long-term placement for your child. It is important for the center to be close enough to your home so you can visit easily. Again, it is important for the people in charge to know about your child's physical and psychiatric condition, recognize and use his strengths, know his treatment plan, and monitor the effects of his medication.

## Conclusion

I have given you a brief summary of the more common mental

illnesses and their treatment. There is so much information to learn about these different illnesses that it is impossible for one doctor to be an expert in all fields, so try to select one who is an expert in the illness affecting *your* child. It is important that you always remember that you did not cause your child's illness and find professionals who understand this. It will make a tremendous difference in how your child's case is managed and the part you play in his progress.

Keep in mind that this chapter, and this book, is only one resource, you will need to continue to learn and the Reading List at the end of this book is a good place to start. Another place to find both information and support is a family support group. This is covered in more detail later in the book, but I heartily recommend joining a group as an excellent way to learn, to get comfort, to find guidance from people who understand what you are going through. Eventually you might be able to help others who will be facing what you have already faced.

## REFERENCES

American Psychiatric Association. *Diagnostic and Statistical Manual of Mental Disorders*. 3d ed., rev. Washington, D.C.: American Psychiatric Association, 1987.

Egeland, J.A., D.S. Gerhard, D.L. Pauls, J.M. Sussex, K.K. Kidd, C.R. Allen, A.M. Hostetter, and D.E. Housman. "Bipolar affective disorders linked to DNA markers on chromosome 11," *Nature* 325 (February 26, 1987): 783–87.

Erikson, E. *Childhood and Society*. 2d. ed. New York: W.W. Norton & Company, 1950.

Chess, S. and A. Thomas. *Annual Progress in Child Psychiatry and Child Development*. New York: Brunner/Mazel, 1981.

Gold, M.S. with L.B. Morris. *The Good News About Depression: Cures and Treatments in the New Age of Psychiatry*. New York: Villard Books, 1987.

Gould, M., R. Wunsch-Hitzig, and E. Dohrenwend. "Formulation of hypotheses about the prevalence, treatment, and prognostic significance of psychiatric disorders in children in the United States." In *Mental Illness in the United States*, edited by E. Dohrenwend. New York: Praeger, 1980.

Harding, C.M., J. Zubin, and J.S. Strauss. "Chronicity in Schizophrenia: Fact, Partial Fact, or Artifact?" *Hospital and Community Psychiatry* 38, no. 5 (1987): 477–86.

Kashani, J.H. and G.A. Carlson. "Seriously Depressed Preschoolers." *American Journal of Psychiatry* 144, no. 3 (1987): 348–50.

Knitzer, J. *Unclaimed Children*. Washington, D.C.: Children's Defense Fund, 1982.

Links, P.S. "Community Surveys of the Prevalence of Childhood Psychiatric Disorders: A Review." *Child Development* 54 (1983): 531–48.

Lourie, I.S. and J. Katz-Levy. "Severely Emotionally Disturbed Children and Adolescents." In *The Chronically Mentally Ill*, edited by Menninger. Washington, D.C.: American Psychiatric Association Press. In Press.

McKnew, D.H., L. Cytryn, and H. Yahraes. *Why Isn't Johnny Crying? Coping with Depression in Children*. New York: W.W. Norton & Company, 1983.

Mirsky, A.F., E. K. Silberman, and S. Nagier. "Follow Up Study Adult Outcomes of High Risk Children: Differential Effects of Town and Kibbutz Rearing." *Schizophrenia Bulletin* 11 (1985): 150–54.

Papolos, D.F. and J. Papolos. *Overcoming Depression*. New York: Harper and Row, 1987.
Robins, L. "Psychiatric Epidemiology." *Archives of General Psychiatry* 35 (1978): 697–702.
Taube, Carl A. and Sally A. Barrett, eds. *Mental Health, United States* 1985. Washington, D.C.:
    U.S. Department of Health and Human Services, 1985.
Torrey, E.F. *Surviving Schizophrenia: A Family Manual*. New York: Harper and Row, 1983.

## Parent Statements

No one answered a single question. I was left in the hospital halls like leftover towels. It was as if I didn't exist. I was so scared. I had never seen anybody act so crazy before and it was my kid. I didn't know what to do.

I thought the pain would never go away and it hasn't. Not completely, but I've learned to live with it. I have to. My son needs me to work with the professionals for him since he can't.

We spent years trying to find out what was the matter with Kim. We went from one doctor to another and most of them told us it was all our fault. We tried every kind of family therapy going. We turned ourselves inside out. I carried Kim for two weeks because they told me I wasn't giving her enough love and she needed to be in constant physical contact with me. My husband and I spend endless agonizing hours dissecting our marriage, riddled with guilt over a child we had been told was only reacting to our latent hostility to each other.

All those terms are so confusing. I have never understood what schizophrenia is. Is it mental illness or emotional disorder, or disturbance or what? It's hard enough to try to deal with what's happening to your child and then to have to figure out some new language is too much.

═❦═

Eventually we were told that Kim was hyperactive and had deep emotional problems that had nothing to do with us. I suppose it should have made us feel better, but by then we were so conditioned to feeling guilty that we refused to believe it. It took us years more to accept that we weren't bad people and even now we still have times where we accept guilt that doesn't belong to us.

═❦═

I saw Dr. Torrey on the Donohue Show. They posted the sign about the Alliance for the Mentally Ill during the show. I called them to see if they could tell me about a good doctor to take my seventeen-year-old daughter to. She was fine until three months ago when she refused to go to school, dress, eat, or go out of the house. She talks to people who aren't there. She's up all night. She rarely sleeps. I can't leave her alone at all. She was in the state hospital for three months. The people at the hospital told me she was a hopeless case. Is she? I need some help.

═❦═

When my sister became ill I felt very sorry for her because she changed so completely and seemed to have no control over this change. The longer she stayed ill, the more I began to believe that her condition was hopeless. I couldn't stand the thought of her living her life in a mental institution and the thought of her always being paranoid and frightened by delusions. Yet there seemed to be no treatment that had permanent good results. After three years she got a new combination of drugs that worked. She's been well now for four years and I finally think that it'll last. It's wonderful to go to sleep without nightmares and to know that my sister isn't going to go through life being tortured by her own thoughts.

I guess doctors do the best they can but people are used to thinking that mental illness is something you can cure yourself of if you just have enough will power and doctors are only people. I can understand that. What I can't understand is why they seem to think it's our fault. I mean, we love our children, all three of them. Just cause Ben is sick doesn't mean we don't love him.

When our teenaged son got sick we were frantic. He lay in bed all the time. He didn't eat and he talked about death and how worthless he was. We couldn't understand; we had always loved him and been so proud of him. We couldn't believe he didn't know how important he was to us. We were lucky, though. He was in the hospital being treated for depression and the staff psychiatrist said it was just environmental and if we could learn to talk together it would all go away. I just couldn't believe it, so I started doing some research and he has a severe clinical depression and is being treated with Lithium. And it's working, that's why we're so lucky. All of a sudden we have our son back.

After a six-week workshop session for families aimed at helping them understand mental illness, a father said, "Thanks so much. My daughter is fourteen and has had schizophrenia for five years. This is the first time that someone told me what it is."

I feel so guilty. Johnny's biological father was an alcoholic and was eventually placed in a state hospital where he died. Johnny had a tough childhood. I feel so guilty. I should have protected him more. My second husband won't have anything to do with Johnny. I feel torn. You know, you can't just talk to anyone about your son's mental illness. People just don't understand.

If it's true that a lot of mental illness is caused by something wrong in the genes, then that's hard enough to handle. After all, we gave our kids their genes and it hurts to know we gave them something wrong, but we didn't do it on purpose. A whole lot of therapists seem to think we tortured our kid or something. That somehow we caused all this. There's not much sympathy for the parents, that's for sure.

=✹=

*A Silent Cry . . .*
A little child cries, Mommy please help me . . .
The mother tries, she prays and she cries,
    only red tape to find.
Words are spoken, unknown to her; directions
    are given, to places she has never heard of.
A mass of confusion, such a new world, she thinks,
    if I'd done better and passed my health
    would I know what a brain dysfunction was?
Her family is slowly falling apart, seems no one
    understands what is so strongly impressed upon
    her heart . . .
No one to turn to, no place to go; her head feels
    like jello, her life seems going to hell.
How can she beat the system, to let her child live?
You are PROFESSIONALS who can help, please step in,
    extend your hand and try to understand that people
    will listen to you, when the mother can't win.
Voice the child's needs to those that will hear; make
    it possible for the little child to live.

                                          Beth Smith

# TWO
## ═✻═

# The Beginning Stages

### EVELYN McELROY, PH.D.

Although the reality you are facing is probably overwhelming for you, it might help to know that you are not alone. About fifteen million parents have gone through what you are going through right now. They, too, have had to face mental illness in their children.

While experts are able to give us these figures, what they can't do is determine when these illnesses begin and predict how long they will last. Parents too often have trouble identifying when, and if, their child has a mental disorder. Every child is different and with each child the number and severity of the symptoms may vary. In some cases, the beginning stages of mental illness happen slowly, over a long period of time, and parents are confused as to whether their child is behaving within the boundaries of "normal" behavior or not. In other cases, the early stages are sudden, and the symptoms strong enough for immediate concern.

The following story will give you an example of how one family tried to gauge their child's sudden change in behavior patterns. The problems they faced and the steps they took are fairly typical of parents in this situation.

## The Beginning Of A Mental Illness

*The students at St. Vincent's were hurriedly stashing their belongings in their lockers and grabbing school supplies necessary for the first class of the day. The school principal announced over the intercom that it was time for the students to turn in the money col-*

*lected from raffle tickets sold to raise money for the high school. She also added that the student selling the most tickets would be listed in the school paper and be considered for "student of the month." She ended with, "Have a good day and God bless you."*

*Lisa Watson, a senior with four months left before graduation, slammed the door of her locker, turned to her best friend and said that she was, "Not going to take that _____ anymore. I'm going to do something about how this _____ _____ school is run."*

*She stormed down the hall to the Vice Principal's office, informed the secretary that she wanted to see Sister Mary and waited for a response. Sister Mary was busy.*

*So Lisa bolted past the secretary, kicked the door open and shouted in a rapid jumble of words, "I didn't come here to sell raffle tickets and I'm not going to do it now or ever! The student paper sucks. I'll wear alligator socks if I want to. Name pins are stupid. Who cares who the student of the month is? Library passes are worse and I'll use whatever door I want to enter the English resource room! Your policies are sick and Sister Catherine (the principal) is having a nervous breakdown."*

*Lisa then left the office and invaded two different classrooms in an attempt to rescue her friends from teachers whom she felt were menacing them. Finally she left school, caught the bus, and returned home.*

Lisa's parents were faced with a very difficult problem. How could they decide if their daughter's behavior was a one time outburst or the beginning of symptoms of mental illness? They were facing the same dilemma that millions of us have faced. The Watsons had to consider the same things all of us have to consider when deciding if our children have a mental illness.

## Does My Child Have A Mental Illness?

Determining if your child's behavior is normal or abnormal is very difficult because she is not an adult and does not follow adult guidelines.

We've all met people who exhibit behavior different from that of most other people we know. Many of these individuals are interesting, offbeat characters, but function within our normally accepted guidelines. Judging behavior solely on the basis of its rarity can be misleading. In fact, many people take pride in not being "normal." It can be an advantage for a fashion model to be taller than average; being smarter than average has obvious merit; and good looks are frequently an asset in our culture. Being too tall, too smart, and too beautiful are all hallmarks of being abnormal—in a positive sense.

The question becomes how do you distinguish socially acceptable but unusual behavior in your child, from actions that suggest mental illness? If your child's behavior is grossly disorganized, makes little sense in her surroundings, and is poorly understood by most of the people with whom she has dealings, then she may be mentally ill. Under these circumstances, you should seek professional help in assessing if she has a mental illness.

## Areas of Assessment

It is possible that your child's actions are within that gray area that makes a decision difficult and you are not sure if she needs professional help or not. Use the following list to help you decide whether or not you need to have your child professionally evaluated. We will use some of Dr. Michael Rutter's areas of assessment from his book *Helping Troubled Children* to describe how some experts estimate a youth's mental status:

1. Is this behavior normal?
2. Does this behavior persist?
3. Is this behavior appropriate for the child's age and sex?
4. Have there been changes in the child's life?
5. What is the child's socio-cultural setting?
6. What is the extent of the disturbance?
7. How severe and frequent are the symptoms?
8. Do these symptoms occur in more than one situation?
9. How impaired is the child?

### 1. Is This Behavior Normal?

*The first clue that something was wrong with Lisa was the* drastic change in behavior *that the outburst at school signified. Lisa was a bright, popular, attractive teenager. She had never*

*shown rude or aggressive behavior toward school authorities. Fur-*
*thermore, her actions were outside the bounds of what is considered*
*merely "assertive." Lisa's behavior was much different from her*
*usual temperament. The second clue was to see if the problem*
*persisted.*

## 2. Does This Behavior Persist?

Actions that are alien to someone's usual way of responding to
events may occur occasionally in anyone and be chalked up to a bad
day. There is no reason to be overly concerned if the behavior does
not last long and does not have long lasting repercussions. On the
other hand, troublesome behavior that remains for a period of time
is more of a cause for concern. This behavior can interfere with school,
friendships, and family life. You have to evaluate how well your child
is doing in school, with friends, and at home. All of these areas are
important to normal developmental growth.

> *Since Lisa managed to get home and appeared to be relating*
> *to others in her usual manner following the uproar she caused at*
> *school, it seemed that her outrageous behavior was a one time*
> *episode. However, Lisa needed to be observed for a period of time*
> *in order to judge whether or not this behavior was persisting. Her*
> *parents were sufficiently alarmed by what they heard from the*
> *principal to make an appointment with a psychiatrist to see Lisa*
> *as soon as possible, which was two days later. In the meantime,*
> *Lisa's parents needed to assess the appropriateness of Lisa's ac-*
> *tions in regard to her age and sex.*

## 3. Is This Behavior Appropriate for the Child's Age and Sex?

Many behaviors are normal at one age but not another. Having
a temper tantrum at bedtime may be fairly normal for your three year
old, but having one directed at a school principal when you are seventeen is not. There are gender differences in the way that people behave
but the behavior of boys and girls overlap to a large degree. Lisa's
actions were not considered appropriate for her age for either boys
or girls.

You need to observe your child for a period of time in order to
decide if her behavior is presenting obstacles to making friends, progressing in school, or functioning in your family. If you do observe

problems, then you want to determine the degree of your child's social impairment. So far, Lisa's behavior did seem to be within the broad range of actions of an angry teenager. And it did not seem to persist. Next, the Watsons needed to look at the changes facing Lisa to see if mounting pressure might have played a role in her angry outburst.

### 4. Have There Been Changes in the Child's Life?

Significant changes in your child's life such as a move to a new school, the birth or death of a loved one, or an illness can disrupt her developmental growth. These and other events can increase anxiety and upset her mental balance temporarily and produce behavioral difficulties. These are to be expected. With time and your support, your child will probably adapt to her new circumstances.

*But nothing unusual had happened to Lisa lately. She had been selected for a leading role in her school play. She had been in several previous plays so this leading role was not a totally new experience for her. Her graduation, just a few months away, could be a source of stress. However, she had made plans for college and was looking forward to going. She had been functioning well. The Watsons decided that they needed to look elsewhere for further clues.*

### 5. What is the Child's Socio-Cultural Setting?

There are many cultural variations in behavior expressed in our society. People from backgrounds other than the majority may face difficulties when they express themselves in ways that appear peculiar to those without similar backgrounds. Their behavior may be normal for their background. The key is to try to understand both the person's past behavior and the typical behavior of those in his socio-cultural setting. If the person is behaving strangely both in terms of his normal behavior and the normal behavior of those with a similar cultural background, then there is cause for concern.

*Lisa was of Irish background, was Protestant, attended a Catholic school and her father was a dentist. Her mother was a physical therapist. Lisa's behavior at school was not typical of those with similar backgrounds or of her classmates. The Watsons needed to mark this as another area of concern. Now they had to try to learn the extent of Lisa's disturbance.*

## 6. What is the Extent of the Disturbance?

A child who is confused about who he is, where he is, and why he is involved in his current activity can be expected to have difficulty in school, problems making friends, and requires extra attention from family members in order to accomplish the everyday tasks of living. He is showing many symptoms of emotional disturbance.

*Lisa didn't fit into that category. Her initial outburst didn't last long and she seemed fairly normal when she arrived home. Possibly the event would never happen again. But her mother was alarmed by several things that happened after Lisa got home.*

## 7. How Severe and Frequent are the Symptoms?

*When Mrs. Watson went to Lisa's room, she found Lisa sitting on the floor rocking back and forth to the beat of loud music. Her posters had been removed and turned to face the wall. "Why are the pictures off the wall?" "Because last night they started to move and talk to me," replied Lisa. Lisa's mother sat down, took a few deep breaths, and thought to herself, "This can't be happening to me." "What?" she asked. "They were moving and noisy! They scared me, so I put them that way so I wouldn't see them."*

*Lisa's comments suggested a severe disorder that required evaluation by a psychiatrist. The frequency and severity of Lisa's symptoms now had appeared both at home and at school and it was obvious that she needed medical attention. Her behavior could be indicative of a variety of psychiatric or medical disorders. The most important thing for the Watsons was to get a diagnosis for Lisa's condition. Once they had a diagnosis, treatment could be prescribed for her.*

*The immediate question the Watsons faced was, "Could Lisa's evaluation wait for two days until her appointment with a psychiatrist or did she require immediate hospitalization in a psychiatric unit?" Although the Watsons were alarmed, they decided to wait the two days. In the meantime they needed to find out if Lisa's problem behavior only occurred in specific situations.*

## 8. Do the Symptoms Occur in More Than one Situation?

A problem which occurs in many or all settings is a more serious disorder than one that only occurs in one situation.

*Later that evening, David and Donna Watson were alarmed to find Lisa talking on the telephone, shouting at the operator and accusing her of interfering with her calls. In reality, she could not manage to dial any of the numbers she wished. Her behavior was verbally abusive to the operator and she seemed very hyperactive. She would not sit down with her parents to discuss the problem. She charged through the house kicking furniture and swearing at all those who got in her way. She did manage to say that the reason she was so angry with the operator was that she had received some messages through the window that she was to call certain people to give them important messages. Lisa felt that the operator knew that and was working against her.*

*With Lisa out of control and her behavior getting worse, the Watsons decided to call a psychiatrist recommended by their family doctor. The psychiatrist suggested that they take Lisa to the emergency room of the nearby general hospital to be evaluated for admission. Since Lisa's behavior was not triggered by any specific situation and was exhibited in several areas, it was apparent that this was a psychiatric emergency. It was now necessary to learn how impaired Lisa was as a result of the abnormality.*

### 9. How Impaired is the Child?

Judging behavior in terms of its abnormality simply means deciding how rare it is. This gives some measure of its significance, yet it is also necessary to ask whether the behavior is doing any harm. Rutter indicates that the degree of suffering, the social restrictions, the interference with development, and the effects on others all must be considered to determine if a mental illness is causing impairment in your child.

Now that you have gone through Dr. Rutter's list on your own and have decided that your child needs further evaluation, the next step is for you plan what to do next.

## Making A Plan

Although your world seems turned upside down, it is important that you get help for your child as soon as possible. Early treatment is very important in order to improve the outlook for your child's illness. You will need to know what is the matter with your child, and what to do about it. You must start planning immediately.

The Watsons were concerned enough about Lisa's behavior to develop a plan to address the problem. They offered more emotional support to Lisa right after the incident. Her mother gathered facts on Lisa's current feelings and psychological state. They made an appointment for the earliest possible psychiatric evaluation. This plan was built on an outline the family used for most health problems. The outline had worked for them in the past, so they applied it to this newest health problem.

They expanded this plan to include their younger daughter, Amy. Lisa's scene at school had embarrassed her. Amy had stayed in school after her sister left and had had to deal with all the questions raised by her classmates who had heard about the uproar. The Watsons had to concentrate on Lisa's needs but they tried to acknowledge Amy's feelings too.

Part of this family plan was to keep the news of Lisa's behavior from friends and family members. We know that there is a stigma attached to mental illness and the Watsons were trying to avoid that stigma both for Lisa and themselves. But in trying to keep Lisa's illness a secret, they were probably adding to their distress. If they don't reach out to others and enlist their support, they will be preventing their loved ones from reacting in the helpful, caring, supportive ways that the Watsons so desperately need now that the family is in crisis.

The Watsons followed their family plan and called the psychiatrist when Lisa's behavior became unbearable. She told them to take Lisa to the emergency room of a local general hospital.

## Taking Your Child To The Hospital

Taking your child to a psychiatric hospital is terrible. You are scared and bewildered, but there are things you can do to make it easier for all of you.

*David and Donna were devastated but surprisingly, they had little trouble convincing Lisa that she needed to see a psychiatrist. In fact, she had always viewed them as interesting people and had once written an essay about them entitled "People I Most Admire." She went with her parents willingly enough.*

*Lisa and Donna sat on wooden chairs in the emergency room while David provided the clerk with the insurance forms and a brief history of the reasons for their visit.*

*After a short while, a tired looking, middle-aged man wearing a white suit and long, white lab coat walked into the examining area. He sipped his coffee, scratched his beard, leaned his elbow against the wall and appeared to be observing Lisa. It was 11:30 P.M.*

*Lisa was sitting on the chair grasping her favorite possessions—David Bowie albums and posters from her room. She watched the doctor watching her.*

*"Well, what are you staring at?" Lisa asked him.*

*"Nothing," he said. "Do you think I'm looking at you?" he asked in return.*

*"Yeah," she said.*

*"I'm Dr. Doe, why don't you come back here and tell me about what is going on with you?"*

*Lisa got up and carried her posters and four David Bowie albums into the examining room. She and the doctor were gone about ten minutes. Then the doctor told David and Donna that he was going to have the nurse evaluate Lisa for possible admission. He reassured them that the nurse had special training and education in the field of psychiatric and mental health nursing.*

The nurse took the Watsons to the psychiatric unit of the hospital. The unit was different from the rest of the hospital in that the door was always locked and the staff wore street clothes rather than uniforms. They passed through the large waiting room located near the circular nurses' station. From here the nurses could see what was happening in most areas of the unit. They were seated in a smaller room and the nurse introduced herself, explained the policy concerning admissions and how the unit operated. She said, "We operate on the team concept here. Everybody participates in the care of the patient. We have a house doctor here who will order the medication and we have a psychiatrist who will see Lisa tomorrow. She will get the medication she needs tonight to get some sleep. We also do routine drug screens to see if the mental problems might be caused by taking street drugs."

Remember, although the team concept of providing patient care means that everyone on the treatment staff of the hospital participates in the development of your child's treatment plan, active psychiatric treatment *requires* that the treatment be directed by a physician. A psychiatrist or child psychiatrist has advanced training in working with people who have mental disorders. It is essential that the psychiatrist have sufficient knowledge and experience with the patient to be able to direct the other members of the team.

Availability of psychiatrists in hospitals varies. Some psychiatrists meet for substantial periods of time with the patient and provide appropriate therapy. Some hospitals may employ physicians to merely meet with other team members who actually provide the "hands on" care while he consults with them.

It is in your child's best interests to have a well-qualified psychiatrist with successful experience in dealing with your child's condition . Unfortunately, some hospitals employ insufficient numbers of psychiatrists to effectively direct treatment. This is something you should consider when helping to plan your child's treatment.

> *For the Watsons, Lisa's behavior was an emergency and they took their psychiatrist's advice and checked their daughter into the hospital.*

## How Do You Get Your Child Admitted Under Emergency Conditions?

The most important thing you need is information. Call a mental health professional you trust to find out what emergency psychiatric resources there are in your community. This is what the Watsons did to get the information they needed to proceed. If you don't know anyone to call, and it's a weekday, call the Department of Mental Hygiene or its equivalent in your state. The telephone operator should be able to give you the phone number. Ask for the division of child and adolescent psychiatry and ask to talk to a professional in that division. The Department of Mental Hygiene should have a wealth of information on both private and public facilities for you.

Another source of information is the Mental Health Association (MHA) or the local chapter of the National Alliance for the Mentally Ill (NAMI). NAMI groups are made up of families of the mentally ill to educate, support, and advocate for the mentally ill and their families. The MHA staff or NAMI families may be able to answer your questions about how to get your youngster connected with a psychiatrist who can screen her and make recommendations. Usually parents have an enormous reservoir of information on effective and ineffective mental health professionals. This informal network is most impressive in providing information in a caring, straightforward manner. A list of the chapters of the NAMI and MHA appears in Appendix B.

If your emergency occurs over a weekend, during the evening, or night, then call the nearest large general hospital and ask for the emergency room. Ask to speak with the head nurse. Tell him that you have a psychiatric emergency that needs to be evaluated and ask where you should go.

If there is a university affiliated hospital in your community, usually it has a department of psychiatry. You could call there and speak with a psychiatrist in training (resident) who is working in the emergency room. He can perform emergency psychiatric assessments and make referrals.

## What If My Child Doesn't Want To Go To The Hospital?

If all your efforts to persuade your child to go to the hospital voluntarily have failed, then you have to consider the procedures for an emergency commitment. This is an extremely stressful procedure for your family since it requires the possible intervention of the legal system. In order for you to commit your child involuntarily to a psychiatric unit, you must check with your state's attorney to find out the law in your state. Generally the commitment procedure goes like this:

1. Parents are responsible for procuring their children's medical care and are believed to be acting in the best interests of their children. The parents' beliefs and wishes are seriously considered by the legal and medical system.

2. A petition for commitment of your child must be initiated. This usually can be done by you, as her parents. Licensed physicians, licensed psychologists, or other specially designated persons may also initiate the commitment process.

3. You can request a physician, or a psychiatrist to examine your child. States vary on who and how many professionals are required to examine the individual. If the examiner(s) decides that the grounds for commitment exist, then the examiner's

report is attached to your petition for commitment. The petition is then filed with the court.

4. After your petition is filed, a peace officer, usually a policeman, can bring your child to the hospital to be examined by a psychiatrist. Often you can accompany your child to the hospital.

5. The psychiatrist judges whether or not your child meets the criteria for commitment and she is then either admitted to the hospital or released.

6. In most states, an emergency commitment lasts for seventy-two hours. Then you, or the director of the hospital must file another petition with the court requesting a longer commitment, or your child is released. If another petition is filed, then a hearing must be held, either at the hospital or in a courtroom.

   a. The hearing is held before a judge, a similar judicial authority, or a Mental Health Commission.

   b. Your child should be present at the hearing unless a psychiatrist testifies that it would be detrimental to her health.

   c. Your child is represented by either a private or state lawyer.

   d. There may be testimony from examiners of your child, family members, and even your child herself.

You should always be present at these hearings and be prepared to testify. You can never rely on someone else to explain how your family plans to handle your child's illness as well as you can.

Often officials of several different agencies will be present at this hearing to present their plans for your child. These agencies have responsibilities for delivering services to mentally handicapped youngsters, depending on how the child's condition is defined. These agencies include Social Services, Juvenile Service Administration, Mental Health, Developmental Disabilities, and Education. When so many agencies are involved in planning the future of one child it can result in a lack of coordination and chaos. You will have to learn the rules applying to each agency and figure out how to best use their complex bureaucratic systems for the benefit of your child.

## Agencies

The court can decide to give the responsibility for your child to any one of several different agencies. This responsibility can extend through the life of her involuntary commitment to a psychiatric hospital into her return to the community. Whichever agency has responsibility for your child, it is this agency that will determine where your child is placed, what her treatment will be, and what role you can play in her immediate future. With such power, it is essential that you understand what these agencies are, and what they do.

The Social Services Administration (SSA) is an agency usually located in the State Department of Human Resources (DHR). This agency has the responsibility for children decided by the court to be "children in need of assistance" (CINA). These children are often abandoned, abused, dependent, neglected or mentally handicapped with parents who are unable or unwilling to care for them. SSA arranges and pays for boarding care with foster parents or places children in public group facilities. Some of these children may be placed in private residential facilities funded to a limited extent by SSA.

The Juvenile Service Administration (JSA) serves troubled children who have been judged by the court to require medical assistance. The JSA is often located within the State Department of Health or Mental Health/Hygiene (DHMH). This agency primarily serves children designated as delinquent or "children in need of supervision" (CINS). The children are usually truant, disobedient, and ungovernable. A delinquent is a minor who has committed an act that would be a crime if committed by an adult. The juvenile court may commit a child involuntarily to a psychiatric facility if it determines that the child is a CINA, a CINS, or a delinquent *and* that the child:

1. Has a mental disorder.
2. Needs inpatient medical care for the protection of himself or others.
3. Is unable to be voluntarily admitted to a facility.
4. No less restrictive treatment alternative exists.

Mentally retarded children who are also mentally ill may be served by yet another agency, the Developmental Disability Section (DDS). This agency is often a branch of the Department of Health and/or Mental Health.

Your state educational system also has responsibility for providing free public education to children and adolescents with mental illness. This mandate comes from the Education for All Handicapped Children Act of 1975 (Public Law 94–142). This is covered more fully in Chapters 5 and 6.

In some states, you must give up custody of your child to get the mental health services your child needs. The Department of Social Services often requires custody before funding treatment of a child. This also happens with the Juvenile Service Administration. Giving up custody of their child places a terrible burden on loving parents who want to help determine treatment choices for their child.

Since having your child committed involuntarily is an emotional nightmare, I urge you to try your hardest to find some way to get your child to agree to being hospitalized. Your psychiatrist may have some creative ideas on ways to appeal to your child that would work.

## Planning The Trip To The Hospital

After your child agrees voluntarily to go to the hospital, you must *develop a plan on how to proceed*. Take another adult member of your family or a friend with you. This is a family crisis and you will need help from some supportive person. Have someone else drive so that you can concentrate on your child. This is a stressful time for both of you and you want to make things as easy as possible for your child.

Ask yourself if there is a special toy or any objects that can be easily and quickly obtained that your child will find comforting if the physician decides to admit her to the hospital.

Bring your insurance identification card and any other pertinent medical information such as the name of your child's pediatrician.

Be sure to tell your child where you are taking her, why you are doing it, and what she can expect in the emergency room. Explain that she will see a doctor who will ask her some questions about how she is feeling. Reassure her that the doctor will be trying to learn of ways to help her get through this period of distress. Emphasize that you will be involved with your child's treatment and that you are sure that the situation can be worked out so she will feel better.

Then, go quickly to the emergency room. Delaying adds more pressure for everyone. Have the driver let you out near the entrance and accompany your child to the admitting area. The driver can join you later. You want to reduce as much extra time and outside stimulation from the surroundings as possible. Your child is usually in a fragile psychological state and her possible admission to a psychiatric unit may upset her initially. Later, she usually finds hospitalization beneficial since other patients and staff may help her see that her problems are not unique. She may come to feel hopeful because she senses that her problems are being addressed and may be solved.

*It had been a long, horrible night for the Watsons. They had had to leave their daughter in a hospital and trust strangers to care for her. They had reassured Lisa that they would be back the next day and then they had gone home to turn their attention to Lisa's sister, Amy.*

## How The Family Copes

*The Watsons did their best to comfort their other child. They reassured her that Lisa was getting the best possible care, that she was content where she was, and that as her parents, they were confident that Lisa could be helped.*

*Donna and David dropped into bed exhausted. Their emotions were in turmoil. They were both worried about Lisa and both felt responsible for causing her illness. They had started feeling guilty just as most parents feel guilty in the same situation.*

Any time a loved child has a serious illness, parents may experience feelings of guilt. Parents of children with leukemia talk about having these feelings. So do parents who have lost children to crib death. So do parents of children with a sudden serious mental illness. Parents don't cause leukemia or crib death and you didn't cause your child's illness either.

There is no evidence from well controlled studies that families cause schizophrenia, major depressions, autism, or any of the other major mental illnesses. On the contrary, most evidence is that no one knows what causes these illnesses. Much research has been directed recently to biochemical causes of major mental illness, rather than faulty child rearing practices. Incredible as it may be, there are still some professionals who do believe that parents cause these psychiatric disorders in their children. They may use these theories to guide the treatment of your child. These professionals often view the families as patients who are sick and in need of therapy rather than allies who are deeply affected by their child's illness. They will treat you as the problem rather than using you as one of the tools to help your child. You must screen your professionals carefully for the best possible results for your child and for your family.

*The Watson household was in a state of crisis. They were tense, upset, distressed, and in a state of shock. They needed to be told what was the matter with Lisa and what they could do about it. They did not cause Lisa's illness, they were not to blame for it, and they should not feel guilty in any way. What they should do is try to work with Lisa's professional team in helping her get better. But first they had to confront their own feelings.*

*David commented that ". . . these things happen to other people. Not to us! Not to people who have always loved their daughters and made every effort to provide for their well being. I would have opted for major dental coverage in my insurance plan rather than psychiatric care if given a choice. Who would have thought we would have needed it?"*

*Amy kept repeating, "I can't believe it. I can't believe this would happen to Lisa."*

*The Watsons were in the beginning stages of a grief reaction. A grief reaction occurs at the loss of someone valued, such as when someone dies. It also occurs when someone you love changes drastically in personality so that you can scarcely recognize the new person. Donna felt that the Lisa they knew was gone. Her spontaneity, humor, laughter, and characteristic ways of engaging life had been taken over by a stranger. They looked alike; that was all. Lisa was missing and her family wanted her back.*

The Watsons felt this grief and extreme distress because of the psychological loss of Lisa combined with the seriousness of her condition; not because they were upset about separating from her. Some mental health professionals claim that a mental illness results from a conscious or unconscious wish of the parents and child to remain together "unnaturally" as a family unit. Efforts for the adolescent to leave results in a severe form of separation anxiety because the parents will not let the child go. These professionals claim that the adolescent is caught in this psychological tug of war with the parents. This tug of war results in psychotic behavior on the part of the adolescent.

This theory discounts the tremendous burden families in crisis face and indicates a lack of understanding of the complex problems they encounter. As a result, families of mentally ill youths sometimes have to contend not only with the burden of their child's illness, but also with insensitive professionals who point the finger of blame at them. This is an unnecessary burden that families don't need.

To respond to the kind of crisis we are describing here, families must plan how they are going to proceed. It is exhausting to cope with the sudden and drastic changes that can occur when your child has a serious illness. First, try to think about people in your life who have helped you through traumatic times in the past. Next, get in touch with them and tell them what has happened. Just reaching out and talking to a helpful person can reduce some of your distress. Keep in mind that your spouse is on the front line just as you are. This kind of crisis deeply affects both of you and therefore limits the amount of energy each of you has to devote to this crisis. Expand your group of supportive persons and don't depend just on each other.

Worries about the stigma of mental illness can prohibit parents from reaching out to others. Your reluctance to talk about your child's problem is a common desire for families who initially face these situations. Keeping such a secret can use a lot of psychological energy and you will need all the energy you can get for the important things to do with your child's care. Hiding your problem can also prevent you from getting the emotional support, understanding, and help you need.

Many Americans still think mental illness should not be discussed. Their attitude tends to get communicated to families and then those family members don't talk about it either. This is dangerous for people in your situation. Secretive behavior can result in physical and emotional isolation. Don't fall into that trap. Reach out to others. At some point you may want to join a support group with other parents who are in a similar situation. The NAMI or MHA networks can inform you of possible groups in your area.

Along with blaming yourself for your child's condition, you may blame your spouse. Although this is a common reaction, I urge you to avoid this because such accusations are often based on the feelings of guilt that we discussed earlier. Parental arguments and discord only increase the anxiety and distress that families are facing at this time. Don't spend your time searching for who is to blame for your child's illness. Spend it planning for her future. Remember, you didn't cause her illness and neither did your spouse.

Get plenty of rest. Don't discuss stressful topics like bill paying and politics before going to bed. You need your rest to cope with the strains of your everyday life. If you exercise, continue with your normal routine as much as possible. These routines have value as stress management aids.

You will be expending a lot of energy in making arrangements for your child's care. Plan to save some time each day to do something you enjoy that relates to your individual interests. Keep in mind that your enjoyment will not be as great as usual due to your current family crisis. But you will feel some temporary relief and you will need all the positive relief you can get. If you try to maintain your emotional balance it will be easier for you to be hopeful. And there is good reason for hope.

## Conclusion

Although no one knows the causes of many of these severe forms of mental illness, most of them can be effectively treated. In some cases, your child may need to be hospitalized to get the treatment she needs. Chapter 3 will look at how to select the right psychiatric hospital for your child.

### REFERENCES

Knitzer, J. *Unclaimed Children*. Washington, D.C.: Children's Defense Fund, 1982.
President's Commission on Mental Health. *Report of the President's Commission on Mental Health*. Washington, D.C.: Government Printing Office, 1978.
Robins, L. "Psychiatric epidemiology." *Archives of General Psychiatry* 35 (1978): 697–702.
Gilmore, M. et al. "Defining and Counting Mentally Ill Children and Adolescents." Paper presented at NIMH Workshop on Severely Emotionally Disturbed Children and Adolescents, 1983.
Gould, M. et al. "Formulation of hypotheses about the prevalence, treatment, and prognostic significance of psychiatric disorders in children in the United States." In *Mental Illness in the United States*, edited by E. Dohrenwend. New York: Praeger, 1980.
Lourie, I.S. and J. Katz-Levy. "Severely Emotionally Disturbed Children and Adolescents." In *The Chronically Mentally Ill*, edited by W. Menninger. Washington, D.C.: American Psychiatric Association Press. In press.
Links, P.S. "Community Surveys of the Prevalence of Childhood Psychiatric Disorders: A Review." *Child Development* 54 (1983): 531–48.
Offord, D.R. "Child Psychiatric Disorders: Prevalence and Perspectives." *Psychiatric Clinics of North America* 8 (1985): 637–52.
Rutter, Michael. *Helping Troubled Children*. New York: Plenum Press, 1975.
American Psychiatric Association. *Diagnostic and Statistical Manual for Mental Disorders*. 3d ed. Washington, D.C.: American Psychiatric Association, 1980.
Joint Commission on the Mental Health of Children. *Crisis in Child Mental Health: Challenge for the 1970s*. New York: Harper and Row, 1970.
Lourie, I. et al. *Chronically Mentally Ill Children and Adolescents: A Special Report for the Plan for the Chronically Mentally Ill*. Rockville, MD: National Institute of Mental Health, 1980.
Brands, A. et al. *Training Manual for Health Care Financing Administration Consultant Surveyors of Psychiatric Hospitals*. Baltimore: HCFA 1–12, 1985.
Torrey, E.F. *Surviving Schizophrenia: A Family Manual*. New York: Harper and Row, 1983.
Leviton, S.P. and N.B. Shuger. "Maryland's Exchangeable Children: A Critique of Maryland's System of Providing Services to Mentally Handicapped Children." *Maryland Law Review* 42 (1983): 823–63.

Mirsky, A.F. et al. "Follow Up Study Adult Outcomes of High Risk Children: Differential Effects of Town and Kibbutz Rearing." *Schizophrenia Bulletin* 11 (1985): 150–54.

Maryland Courts and Judicial Proceedings Code Ann §3–801(e),(p) (1980 & Supp. 1982). Md. Ann. Code Art. 88A 61 (b) (I)(i) (1979 & Suppl. 1982).

Maryland Ann. Code art. 88A 60 (1979 & Supp. 1982); Md. Admin. Code tit. 07 02.11.02A (1978).

Md. Ann. Code art. 88A 32C (1979).

Md. Health-Gen. Code Ann. §6–116(a) (1982). Md. Cts. & Jud. Proc. Code Ann. 3–829(b) (1) (1980 & Supp. 1982).

Md. Cts. & Jud. Proc. Code Ann. §3–801 (1) (1980 & Supp. 1982).

Md. Cts. & Jud. Proc. Code Ann §3–801 (k) (1980 & Supp. 1982).

Department of Health and Mental Hygiene v. Prince George's County, 47 Md. App. 436, 447 n.10, 423 A.2d 589, 596 n.10 (1980).

Nuechterlein, K. "Childhood Precursors of Adult Schizophrenia." *Journal of Child Psychology and Psychiatry.* In press.

U.S. Congress. *Education for All Handicapped Children Act of 1975*, P.L. 94–142. Washington, D.C.: Supt. of Docs., U.S. Govt. Printing Office, 1975.

Haley, J. *Leaving Home: The Therapy of Disturbed Young People.* New York: McGraw-Hill, 1980.

Madison, D. and W.L. Walker. "Factors Affecting the Outcome of Conjugal Bereavement." *British Journal of Psychiatry* 1, no. 8 (1967): 1057–76.

# Parent Statements

My problem was how to get him psychiatric treatment. Every time we had an uproar at home because of the way he went around abusing everyone, I'd call the police. They'd come and say, "We don't see that any law has been broken. We can't take him anywhere." They acted like I abused *him* rather than the other way around. I'd have the bruises and cuts and he'd be fine, but it was still my fault because I was the parent and he was the child. Finally last spring, Fred hit me and broke my tooth and split my gums. I charged him with assault and battery. The police took him to jail. The prosecutor began talking about charging him with criminal charges. I said, "Hey, wait a minute, he needs treatment, not jail." Finally they agreed to transfer him to a state hospital where adolescents are treated. The medication he's getting has completely turned him around. He's easier to live with; he's just another person.

═ ✹ ═

After my sister became ill, I became very withdrawn. This was mainly because I felt so depressed it was hard to find the energy to be happy and outgoing when my sister was so sick. At first

I didn't tell any of my friends but eventually I talked with some that I was really close with. They gave me so much support and were so persistent in including me in their activities that I felt really lucky. Without them I'd probably still be sitting around all alone.

═❀═

It was seven o'clock in the morning by the time we finally got Brian safely admitted into a psychiatric hospital. It was an emergency situation; he had suddenly become psychotic and needed help. I was totally exhausted. All I could think of was calling my mother; I needed comforting so badly. I told her how Brian was in the hospital and was hallucinating. That he thought he was God. He was wandering around not sleeping and not making any sense. Do you know what she said? She said, "How awful! What did you do to him?"

═❀═

My daughter didn't want to go out at all. It was like she was punishing herself because her brother was in the hospital. I tried to push her to go to her prom but she refused. She told me that she had always been jealous of her brother and now he was sick. She thought it was her fault that he had a breakdown.

═❀═

When I told my parents that Lee was in the hospital, they were just wonderful. They flew out right away and just took over with all the everyday things that still needed to get done—groceries, laundry, just everything. We were able to spend almost all our time in the hospital with Lee. I think it made a difference to Lee too, when she got better and was able to understand what we said about her grandparents being there to help. She knew that everyone loved her and wanted to help her get better.

═❀═

I was chasing my eighteen-year-old daughter down the street. It was real bad for me 'cause I'm fifty myself and my heart's not too good. But I had to do something; she was out of touch with reality. I was afraid of what would happen to her so I tried to get her to come back home but she wouldn't. She was all dressed up in some outlandish clothes. She had on a wrinkled, dirty dress, red nylons and ballet slippers. She had on this weird, dark makeup and it was splashed all over her face. She said she was going to hear the Rolling Stones downtown. If she went downtown like that, we'd all be in trouble.

=❀=

Anyway, she bolted from the house and ran toward the bus line. When I finally caught up with her, she started hitting me. A car stopped and the driver said for me to stop hitting her or he would call the cops! I finally got her home and next day we put her in the hospital to get her stabilized.

=❀=

Once Karen called from the hospital and she sounded all confused and scared. She kept asking if I was all right; if her mother was all right? Then she asked me to come give her a hug. It had to be me. She was crying. It broke my heart to tell her that I couldn't come; visiting hours were over. I always remember that now. It was the blackest time. Sometimes I get up from the dinner table just to give her another hug. Now that she's home, it seems like I have so many hugs to make up for.

=❀=

Chris was only ten when he went into the psychiatric unit five months ago. He had tried to kill himself. The doctors told me that he was severely depressed about the death of his grandfather, and us moving to a new city. I love him and worry about him all the time. But his father left and there's nothing I can do about that. Now I have to work two jobs to make enough and I just don't seem to have the energy to take care of him at home. The social worker at the hospital thinks it would be better for Chris to go to a residential treatment center for a while. It makes sense. I feel so guilty about not being able to have him at home but I feel relieved too. I'm just so glad that the people at the hospital could understand and help. It makes all the difference.

≡❧≡

That first psychiatrist in the hospital was a lifesaver. It was the middle of the night but he sat there for hours explaining just what was happening to David, what we should do, and what he thought would happen next. I couldn't have asked for more.

≡❧≡

Sarah made some really good friends in the hospital. Some patients and some staff. She had to go back for a while once and after her medications stabilized her, she went around like it was a summer camp catching up on all the gossip. We felt terrible that she had to be in the hospital but so relieved that there was some place that could help her.

≡❧≡

Bill has been in and out of hospitals for years now. That's part of our life with his schizophrenia. Since his father's job means we move a lot, I've had a chance to see five or six different hospitals and let me tell you, they can be very different. One is like a resort. My other son wanted to go there, too. He figured it was a lot better than junior high at home. But some of them! It could have been a way station to nowhere. Just patients sitting around staring at nothing. There was no schooling, no activities, and no one seemed to care. I got Bill out of there as fast as I could, which wasn't fast enough.

≡❧≡

Just going through all the red tape to get your child hospitalized is incredible.

=✻=

My problem was that my ex- husband claimed it was all my fault that Tommy had a mental illness. He was trying to get custody and this was a golden opportunity for him. Sometimes I was tempted to just let him have Tommy and good luck to him. Let him hassle with the schools, fight the courts, and fill out all those forms.

=✻=

Since Mary got sick, I've started noticing how people think about mental illness. The difference is fantastic. Some people think they should be chained up somewhere and others know that it is a physical disease. And all those people end up working in the hospital where your kid is. You have to be careful all the time to see that your child gets the right people taking care of her.

=✻=

THREE

# Selecting a Psychiatric Hospital

EVELYN McELROY, PH.D.

If your child needs treatment in a psychiatric hospital, you will have many things to consider. If you have the time to comparison shop for the best hospital for your child's needs, it's a good idea to do so.

This chapter will tell you what things to look for in a psychiatric hospital and how to evaluate care and costs. Keep in mind that hospitalization is very expensive and you will probably need to budget your money carefully. We will discuss types of hospitals, how to use insurance benefits, how to visit a hospital for evaluation purposes, and ways to interview hospital staffs to see if this is the right hospital for your child.

If you are looking into private hospitals, remember that they are so expensive that most patients need medical insurance to afford them. If you don't have insurance, you may have to use the public mental health care delivery system. Both public and private hospitals can be overpriced and yet provide substandard care. Some are excellent. There are many factors besides money to consider and we will go into them in this chapter, but the first step is to learn about insurance coverage.

## Medical Insurance

In order for you to learn just what your insurance policy covers, call your insurance agent. Give the agent your policy number, the name of the person whose name appears on the forms and tell him where the subscriber works. If you feel this could be a prolonged phone call, make an appointment to go over the information you need in person. Another way to get information is to call the personnel office of the place where the subscriber works and ask to speak with someone about verifying the benefits of the policy. Ask the insurance agent these questions:

1. What is the amount per day allowed for psychiatric hospitalization?
    a. Does this per day allowance vary according to hospital? Some insurance companies have a list of preferred hospitals for their consumers to use. These are hospitals that may cost less in the community. If you choose another hospital, you will pay the difference out of your own pocket. If your insurance company does have such a list, ask them to mail you a copy.
    b. In addition to this allowance, does your insurance cover other treatments that may appear on the hospital bill? For example, some hospitals charge for the basic fee, which usually covers room and meals, but figure separately for individual and group therapy, occupational therapy, and the like. Parents are expected to pay for the rest from their own resources.
2. Does the insurance policy specify limits on the number of days allowed in a given period of time?
3. Does the policy have a limit on the amount of dollars that you're allowed for psychiatric care in a psychiatric hospital for lifetime coverage? Some policies have a $100,000 lifetime limit and you need to know that since you can spend that very quickly in some hospitals.
    a. Is there a limit per year on the amount that can be spent for outpatient care?
    b. Is there an amount limited per lifetime on an outpatient basis? Some parents must plan for long-term conditions that can soon exhaust their benefits.

After your conversation, send a letter outlining the results of your discussion. This will document the facts as you see them and allow the company an opportunity to clarify anything that they might feel you misunderstood.

## Major Medical Insurance

If you have major medical insurance, it provides coverage for catastrophic medical illnesses. Major medical options extend the basic medical insurance to diseases requiring longer periods of time to treat than allowed under your basic policy. They significantly increase the dollars you are allowed for treatment of your child's condition. If you need the details of your benefits, read your policy and then contact either the personnel office of the subscriber or the insurance company.

If you aren't sure if your child is covered under your policy, talk with your insurance agent. Usually dependents of the insured are covered under the policy. These dependents include the spouse of the policy owner and unmarried children until the end of the calendar year in which they reach the age of nineteen, unless they are enrolled in an accredited educational institution.

You may wish to ask that your child be allowed to remain as a dependent on your policy after he reaches the age of nineteen. Since you have to do this before he reaches nineteen, find out what the procedures are to do this as far in advance as possible.

Disabled dependents are also covered. They may be any child nineteen or over who is incapable of self-support because of a mental or physical incapacity that began prior to the end of the calendar year in which the child became nineteen. Then the child may remain as a covered dependent under the parent's policy indefinitely. In addition, many policies extend coverage to an unmarried child, age twenty-three or over, who is incapable of self-support because of a mental or physical incapability that began while the child was a full-time student covered under the parent's policy and prior to the child reaching the age of twenty-three. The child may remain covered as a disabled dependent indefinitely, but he must reside with, and be dependent upon, the parent.

## Health Maintenance Organizations (HMOs)

You may not have major medical coverage but instead belong to a Health Maintenance Organization (HMO). HMOs are health care plans that cover you for all medical expenses with just a small fee for each service. But many have limited their psychiatric services to short-term, outpatient or inpatient care. Check with your HMO to see exactly what your coverage is and make sure that your child is covered and will remain covered. Sometimes they automatically take a child off the plan when he reaches a certain age.

HMOs have built-in cost cutting incentives. Usually you are restricted to using the group of physicians or other health professionals employed by the HMO. You give up the right to choose your physician and hospital since you are limited to those chosen by the HMO. You may also be subject to pressure from the HMO to avoid using a specialist since they want to keep down the cost.

The HMO health professionals who assess your health problems make every effort to avoid costly hospitalizations. Many HMOs are willing to offer a partial hospitalization benefit in lieu of inpatient care—trading one inpatient day for every two days of partial hospitalization care. This approach of trading outpatient for inpatient care may appeal to you if your child might benefit from community based care.

Whether you belong to an HMO or have major medical insurance, money will still be a factor in deciding on a psychiatric hospital for your child. The chances are that you will be paying for part of his treatment yourself. You must be able to estimate what these costs are and budget yourselves in order to meet these expenses.

Now that you have learned about your insurance coverage and you are making the decision as to where your child will be treated, you need to think about the types of psychiatric hospitals available to you.

## Types Of Psychiatric Hospitals
### Private General Hospitals

Most private general hospitals have psychiatric wards but may not have extensive facilities for prolonged psychiatric care. Many will not admit children because children need a special environment and staff. Some other hospitals will admit adolescents only for short stays. If you are considering a private general hospital, you will have to check on what is available in your area and what their facilities are for psychiatric care. Often these hospitals provide emergency psychiatric care. State hospitals may use them as a screening and brief treatment facility, and thereby reduce admissions to public hospitals.

As we just discussed, some hospitals have allocated a certain number of beds to be used for crisis or psychiatric emergencies. Often they have a contract with a community mental health center (CMHC) that uses the hospital when patients require care not available to them in the community. Unfortunately, crisis beds are few and limited to a forty-eight-hour stay. If your child requires additional treatment, he may be transferred to a ward if there is space and he meets the admission criteria.

Many general hospitals require that the patient voluntarily sign himself in. If he does not do this, they may refuse to accept him. Then you are forced to find another private hospital where they will accept an involuntary patient.

## Private Psychiatric Hospitals

Private psychiatric hospitals can be either non-profit facilities or proprietary (for profit) that specialize in treatment of mental illness. Many of these hospitals specialize in the treatment of children and adolescents. Some of them are excellent, while others are not. You will need to evaluate each possibility on its own merits. Costly down payments are often demanded by these hospitals on admission but many times you can get them to waive this deposit.

If you don't have private hospital insurance, you may have to have your child admitted to a public hospital so you need to find the public facility that is best suited to your child's needs. Too often there is little choice.

## Public Hospitals

Public hospitals vary a great deal in the quality of care. Some are excellent facilities that equal expensive, private hospitals and others are little more than human warehouses. Be sure you investigate the possibilities carefully. If you choose a public psychiatric hospital, be sure that your child will not be placed with adult psychiatric patients. Children and adolescents need special services and specially trained staff.

In addition to state operated public hospitals, many counties operate psychiatric facilities. There are also university psychiatric units which are either state operated or private depending on the status of the university. Generally these units have professionals familiar with current scientific findings in the psychiatric field. They focus on research, teaching, and training. Look into what your county offers, and check your area universities before making a final decision on where your child will be placed. They can be good alternatives to the public or private hospital.

## Cost of Treatment in Public Hospitals

In many states, families are charged for the cost of care for their child in state operated facilities. For example, in Maryland, a proposed bill states that the recipient of services and the chargeable person (usually the parents) are responsible for payment whether the patient was admitted voluntarily, involuntarily, or by court order.

This is an awesome burden to place on families. Years ago such catastrophic illnesses were viewed as state responsibilities since it was recognized that few people had the financial resources to cope with such mammoth bills. As one example of that thinking, tuberculosis sanitoriums were developed by states. Many advocates for the seriously mentally ill claim that the state has the responsibility to provide care for the mentally ill just as persons with other catastrophic illnesses have been cared for.

## Medicaid Waiver

As a result of recent amendments to the Social Security Act, states may be authorized to offer, under a waiver of medicaid statutory requirements, an array of home and community-based services. These are to replace the necessity for your child being institutionalized. You can obtain case management services that will help your child get needed medical, social, educational, and other services. Remember, these services will only be provided to individuals who would otherwise be institutionalized, under the medicaid program at a cost *equal* or *greater than* the cost of maintaining the individuals in the community.

To find out if your state has requested participation in this program, contact the director of your state Department of Human Resources, or the Department of Mental Hygiene. If they can't help you, write:

United States Department of Health and Human Services
Health Care Financing Administration
6325 Security Blvd.
Baltimore, MD 21207

If you are not in the midst of a crisis situation and have the time to survey the possible hospitals for your child, try to get references from both professionals and other families. This is another area where an organization like NAMI or the MHA can help. Another thing to consider in judging a hospital is whether or not it is licensed and accredited.

## Licensing And Accreditation Of Hospitals

Hospitals must be licensed by a state agency empowered to determine if the facility meets state regulations. In addition, many hospitals are accredited by the Joint Commission on Accreditation of Health Care Organizations (JCAH). The JCAH accreditation process evaluates the hospital on health safety, staffing, documentation of services, and many other things. JCAH accreditation *suggests* that the hospital has met minimum standards of care. Hospitals that win JCAH approval usually display their citation prominently on the wall near the entrance to the hospital. Be sure to ask if the hospital you are considering is accredited by the JCAH. While this accreditation does not indicate excellence, it does *suggest* that certain minimal standards are met. The findings of the JCAH surveys are considered privileged information and you may have trouble getting the reports. Keep trying, you are legally entitled to that information.

Hospitals that receive federal dollars from the Social Security Act (Medicare) must be certified as providing active, individualized treatment and having sufficient staff to implement active treatment. In order to keep their certification, these hospitals are usually surveyed annually.

The Health Care Financing Administration (HCFA) is the federal agency responsible for overseeing the surveys of these psychiatric hospitals and determining certification. If you want to get the results of these surveys, you can write your HCFA regional office. The addresses are listed in appendix C. The reports will be able to tell you if the hospital you are considering cannot provide evidence of individualized treatment planning or if it has problems with inadequate staffing.

You will also want to know if the hospital is in a position to provide the specialized care your child needs.

## Taking Into Consideration Your Child's Special Needs

Before deciding on a hospital, you will need to decide exactly what services your child will need. Talk with his assessment team and get their recommendations. Then take a few minutes to look over the "Health Status Checklist" in Appendix F and see where it is relevant to your child. Simply check those items where your youngster has a problem. Keep those items in mind when you inspect a hospital and ask the staff how they handle those specific problems.

## Inspecting The Hospitals

Armed with your insurance information, a review of the types of hospitals available, and the special needs of your child, it is time to take your tours to inspect the hospitals on your list. Here are some points to keep in mind:

1. Make a list of hospitals near your home. The closer the hospital, the more easily you can visit your child.
2. Make an appointment with a staff member. Request a tour of the ward, the grounds, and the cafeteria.
3. Determine whether the hospitals are JCAH accredited.
4. Learn if they are certified for Medicare coverage. If you have Medicaid, ask if they accept Medicaid patients.
5. Ask if they require a cash deposit for admission. Find out if they will waive the fee if you have a sound insurance policy.
6. Ask the amount charged per day for hospitalization. Hospitals vary greatly in their daily fees, ranging from about $140 to $500 *per day*.
7. Find out if the daily rate covers all costs incurred at the hospital. Some hospitals charge separately for therapy sessions, medications, and the like.
8. Ask if there is a school associated with the hospital. Is the school accredited? Are there charges for the school that are separate from other hospital costs?
9. Ask how a person with symptoms similar to those of your child is treated at this hospital. It is important to know if they use a combination of medication and psychotherapy or if they avoid medication. If your child has a major mental illness,

he probably needs both psychoactive medication and psychotherapy. Hospitals that avoid medication would probably be poorly rated and you might want to avoid placing your child there.

10. Ask how they manage patients that get out of control. If they say they use cold wet sheet packs, cross them off your list because they are operating in the dark ages. Hospitals that use large amounts of seclusion and restraints are generally not staffed well. Such procedures are demeaning to patients and may indirectly affect how they react to hospitalization in the future.

11. What is the bed capacity in the ward your child would be in?

12. How many staff members work on the unit per shift? If there is only one person on each shift for thirty patients, it is unlikely that your child would receive active, individualized treatment. In fact, it is possible that such a staffing pattern would jeopardize the safety of the patients.

13. Ask if a psychiatrist will be treating your child. It is important to have a physician assess his physical and mental condition and determine what specific treatment he requires.

14. Ask about social and recreational activities that are available.

15. Tell the hospital that it is important for the team providing the treatment to your child to consider your family goals. Stress that it is essential that the team involve the family since you are eager to help. Tell them that you want access to the treatment team. *Stress the importance of this type of contact in advance of your child's hospitalization.*

Now go back over the Health Status Checklist. Do you have any questions for the hospital? For instance, does your child have a physical handicap in addition to his mental disorder? Are there ramps for wheelchairs? Possibly you are worried about how the staff will respond to your child's suicidal behavior. Or you are worried about having his seizure medication changed. Now is the time to bring up these issues with the staff. Once you have gotten answers to your questions, it is time to begin your tour of the ward where your child would live.

## Touring the Ward

Is the ward clean and attractively furnished? The rooms are usually shared by two to four people and patients should be allowed to bring articles from home. Toys, stereos, and other personal belongings should be evident in wards for young people. Hopefully, you will see few people in their rooms since active treatment implies that the day is planned so that the kids are involved in treatment, school, or activities during the day and evening hours. Since this is when you are likely to tour, you should see mostly empty beds.

Examine the bathrooms to see if adequate toilet supplies are readily available. Do the bars on showers collapse when you apply pressure? Many people have attempted to commit suicide on solid shower bars; collapsible ones are better. Shatterproof glass should be used as a precaution.

Notice whether the placement of the nursing station allows for adequate viewing of the unit. It is important that the staff be able to quickly see what is going on. Most nursing stations have a room nearby that can be used for persons requiring close observation.

Ask if they have a seclusion room. If they do, visit it. Usually these rooms have a small window in the door that allows the nursing staff to check on the patient in seclusion without entering the room. You want to see if the entire room can be seen from outside the door. Some rooms have blind spots that allow the patient to hide from the staff.

Check that the temperature in the ward feels comfortable. Many people on psychoactive medication are very sensitive to hot weather and their response to heat is altered by the drugs they are taking. It is important for the ward to have air conditioning during hot weather.

Are there unpleasant odors? If so, then there may be housekeeping problems. Ask the staff member giving you the tour.

What are the general facilities of the ward? Is water easily accessible? Are there recreational games and television sets available? Your child will be spending all his time in this miniature world and it is good for him to have all the amusements he can.

Observe how the patients appear. Do they seem drugged? Do many of the patients walk around in a stiff, artificial manner? If so, they may be overmedicated. Do the patients seem to be a good mix for your child? If your child is withdrawn and suffering from severe depression, or is actively delusional and hallucinating, then being on a ward where most of the patients are functioning on a higher social level may make him feel inferior.

If there is a school at the hospital, watch it while it is in session.

You can see the class size and how the teachers respond to the students, and also ask questions about the educational program. It can be important to your child for him to continue with his education at this time. He may be able to feel success in this area and it will give him an opportunity to keep in contact with his life outside the hospital.

What kind of food is served in the cafeteria? Is it appetizing, wholesome, and varied? What your child eats is important to you when he is home, and it's just as important while he is hospitalized.

Be very aware of the psychological atmosphere of the ward as you make the tour. Does the staff interact well with the patients? Do they isolate themselves in the nursing station or move among the patients? Is the noise level manageable? Many people with depression and schizophrenia have difficulty with environments that are too stimulating. Do you think the environment is one that your child could handle? If you think there might be times when he needs to retreat to his room to regain his psychological balance, check that the staff allows this.

Let the staff know that you expect to be involved in the treatment of your child. Give them the goals you have that need to be addressed while your child is hospitalized and emphasize that you must be included in the discharge planning. Make sure you will have access to the professionals treating your child since there will be questions you want answered.

Walk around the grounds. Is there enough space for outdoor recreational activities? How is the space enclosed? Some hospitals have beautiful grounds while others have spaces surrounded by high wire fences and barbed wire. Is there play equipment suitable for both young children and adolescents? A lot of young people work off some of their energy and tension through physical activity and it is important that there is some place for them to do this.

After you have decided on a hospital, someone in the hospital financial office will have to check your insurance benefits to see if your child is eligible to be admitted. Often the admission policy requires a down payment even though you have insurance. The down payment can be expensive, but many times the hospital will waive this cash deposit. Be sure to find out what the procedure is at the hospital you choose.

Once everything is settled with the hospital, try to arrange a preadmission appointment for your child (if you think he can handle it) so that he can see the hospital for himself. A preadmission appointment can help him settle into the hospital environment more easily. He can feel that he helped select the hospital and it may make him more ready to work with his treatment team on the problems that required his hospitalization.

## Conclusion

In this chapter we have described how you can approach a preplanned hospitalization for your child. You needed to consider many things. You may feel a little overwhelmed by all this at a time when you are emotionally trying to adjust to your child's illness, but it can be helpful to see how much you can do to make sure your child gets the treatment he needs. The effort you expend now can pay off in immense dividends for the care and long-term outlook for your child. The right treatment, in the right facility, can make a world of difference in how successful your child is in overcoming his illness.

In the next chapter we will discuss what to do while your child is hospitalized, how to understand your child's diagnosis, how the medication and treatment are working, how to evaluate your child's progress, how to participate in the discharge planning, and ways to use community resources to help your child.

### REFERENCES

Annotated Code of Maryland, Crimes and Punishments, Art. 27, § 97, establishes the responsibility of a parent to support a destitute child. Section 104 establishes the responsibility of a child to support destitute parents.

Annotated Code of Maryland, Health General Article, Title 16–Reimbursements and Collections–deals with the establishment of charges for services in the Department of Health and Mental Hygiene (DHMH) facilities and the determination of fees for such care.

Bausell, R.B. and M.A. Rooney. *The People's Medical Society Health Action Kit: How to Evaluate a Nursing Home*. Emmaus, PA: The People's Medical Society, 1985.

Brands, A. et al. *Training Manual for Health Care Financing Administration Consultant Surveyors of Psychiatric Hospitals*. Baltimore: HCFA 1–13, 1985.

Carter, Beth. *Disability Benefits and Employment: Protecting the Rights of Recipients Who Go To Work: A Manual for Community Mental Health, Rehabilitation and Vocational Staff*. Baltimore: State of Maryland, Mental Hygiene Administration, March 1986.

The Code of Maryland Regulations (COMAR) §10.01.02 is the segment of State regulation that deals with charging and the establishment of fees for services.

Hatfield, Agnes. *Consumer Guide to Mental Health Services*. Arlington, VA.: The National Alliance for the Mentally Ill, 1985.

Health Care Financing Administration, HHS §441.300, 42 CFR Ch. IV (10-1-85 edition) discusses the Medicaid waiver, pp. 156–61.

Joint Commission for Accreditation of Hospitals (JCAH). *Accreditation Manual for Hospitals.* Chicago: JCAH, 1987.

Kopolow, Louis E. *Plain Talk About Handling Stress.* Rockville, MD.: USDHHS Publication No. (ADM) 83–502, 1983.

Lin, Eva. *Help Yourself: A Tip Sheet for Families Living With Schizophrenia.* Baltimore: University of Maryland, School of Nursing, mimeographed paper, 1983.

Maryland State Department of Personnel. *Health Insurance News Bulletin III.* Baltimore: Department of Personnel, January 1987.

*Mental Health Reports: Special Report.* "Effects of HMO Boom On Mental Health Examined." Arlington, VA: Capitol Publications, May 21, 1986.

Russell, L. Mark. *Alternatives: A Family Guide to Legal and Financial Planning for the Disabled.* Evanston, IL: First Publications, 1983.

Shane, Scott. "HMOs Revolution in Medicine." *Baltimore Sun* (Oct. 28, 1986): 14a.

Senate of Maryland, Senate Bill No. 206. Introduced by Senator C. Riley (Department of Health & Mental Hygiene). Introduced and read January 26, 1987.

# Parent Statements

The staff at the hospital informed me that Johnny shouldn't come home because we made him sick. They are recommending that he live with his uncle in Florida. They discount our decisions and Johnny's. What makes them think that his uncle's place is better than ours? He is fifteen hundred miles away and nobody on the staff has ever talked with him. Who do they think they are making decisions about our lives and just informing us about them!

The insurance companies can be really tricky. Before you know it your benefits are gone. Just like that! Doesn't anybody warn you or sit down and explain what can happen? Don't make me laugh. So we had to let the state do for Janie and it wasn't such a good experience. If I knew the system, I could have done a lot better and Janie would have been better off but I didn't. These things always seem to happen when you're real low emotionally. I paid premiums for twenty years and I figure they sort of owe me some kind of explanation of what's going on, but they really hide the facts from you, then bingo! No coverage and all they want is for you to get out of their company and quit costing them money.

When we were visiting our daughter, we noticed that it was very hot outside and the ward seemed overcrowded and hot. People were lying on the floors. There were so many people around that it was hard to get out of the locked ward. It took the nurse's aide ten minutes to free herself from the demands of patients at the nursing station to get to us. The patients were complaining about not enough water. It seems the water fountain was clogged. We were concerned about the near panic situation on the unit, the heat, and lack of water. We notified the health department. When we went back the next day, we were told that they already knew about the situation. Nothing was done. Then we called our congressman. He called us back and told us a federal agency was sending a special team to the hospital to investigate our complaint.

=❧=

My parent group was a great help to me when we were making plans to move our son from the university hospital to the state hospital. They were able to tell us all the things to look out for. They told us the state hospital wasn't so bad. They knew people who had gone there and been helped. That made a difference. We had such awful feelings about the state hospital.

=❧=

My mother just couldn't understand what her granddaughter was going through. She kept saying over and over, "I don't know what you mean when you tell me how she's acting in that hospital." A lot of people have old, scary ideas about what a mental hospital is really like. Unfortunately, some of them still exist.

=❧=

Those staff people can have all the degrees they want, but they can't be too smart cause they never ask me what I think or what I know about my own child. Who would know my child better than me? I could help a lot but they won't let me.

My daughter keeps calling me from the hospital. She apologizes all the time for all the horrid things she says she does. She tells me what she has done with the men in the hospital. She cries and says, "I'm awful. I don't deserve to live. I don't want to do those things. But I do." I keep wondering how she would be if she wasn't safe in that hospital.

≡❀≡

If he were well, he wouldn't do those things. People see that he is confused and sick and they take advantage of him. It hurts him and us to see it happening. It hurts me that I can't help him. He isn't just a mental patient. He's my son. People don't realize that he understands what's happening to him.

≡❀≡

Donny is in a state hospital down state. It's a long drive for me to make and I have to take the whole day off work. Naturally, the visiting hours are during the week, which makes it harder. He's been there for a year and a half and is due to come home soon, but I'm a single mother. There's no one to be with him all day so I'm trying to get the hospital to recommend some kind of halfway house or something. With all the red tape involved, I figure Donny'll be out and home for two months before I ever get an answer about that halfway house.

≡❀≡

The staff tried to help, but even within her team they had different ideas about what was wrong with her. Some people said she had never adjusted to being adopted and others said I had never loved her like she was really my own.

≡❀≡

We went through hell getting Margy placed in this one hospital because it had a school set up and she could go on studying. Well, it didn't work out because the medications she had to take kept her practically a zombie. When I complained, nothing was done. She lost a lot of time before she finally got squared away on her medications and was able to start school again. By then it was too late. She didn't want to go into tenth grade at the age of nineteen.

❧

The first time Fred went to the hospital, it was an emergency. I mean he had been running around the house cutting up the furniture with a knife and was threatening to kill us. So we didn't have the time to do any shopping for a hospital. But he's going to be in there for a long time and I guess we'll have to look around and see what's best for him. First though, I just want to sleep for a long, long time without being afraid.

❧

FOUR

# In the Hospital and Returning Home

EVELYN McELROY, PH.D.

There is a whole miniature world called a psychiatric hospital. Here your child will come in contact with a variety of professionals, get a diagnosis as to what her illness is, start a treatment program, and begin the steps necessary to leave the hospital and rejoin her family.

Each child will have his own experience in the hospital. His length of stay will vary from the next child's, his treatment, his professional team, and even his results. But there are many elements in common that all parents have to consider.

Once your child is settled in the hospital you have selected for her, you will have a little more time to work on all the additional paperwork that her illness demands. One of the most important things is to make sure that she continues to be covered under your insurance policy. Although the probability is that her illness will be successfully treated, it may take some time and repeated hospitalizations. For that you will need insurance coverage.

## Working With The Insurance Company

Find out what your insurance company's policy is on having your child covered, then fill out the necessary forms to request that your child be given continuing coverage. If the agent tells you that this kind of coverage is not possible, send a written request to the Executive

Director or President of your insurance company anyway. Occasionally an agent is not familiar with all the policies of his organization. A dated letter to a representative of your insurance company will at least give you accurate information and may even result in getting coverage for your child.

In your letter you will need to justify your request by documenting the need for additional coverage. This documentation may include the number and length of hospitalizations, the severity of your child's illness, the diagnosis, and the prognosis (expected medical outcome). Ask your doctor to write a letter covering those factors. Often your insurance company is well aware of the severity of your child's condition since it has been paying the bills. Remind them of this.

## Checking The Insurance Charges From The Hospital And Staff

You may want to check that your insurance coverage is being properly used. If your insurance company only has a fixed amount of money available for your child's illness, then you want to be certain that every cent is spent as wisely as possible. Examine the itemized insurance statement you get each month. See if the charges seem reasonable. For example, if the itemized statement lists charges for physical therapy and to your knowledge, your child neither needed nor received such services, you would want to question the accuracy of your bill. Similarly, if the psychiatrist charged the insurance company for forty-one visits during your child's ten-day hospitalization, question it.

Remember, your child's medical record is a legal document that is used to record the treatment plan and care she received. If you can find no record of these forty-one visits on your child's medical record, then you can assume that those visits did not occur. Challenge the accuracy of the bill and don't pay for care your child is not receiving.

*Let's see how the Watsons checked on bills from Lisa's private psychiatric hospital that seemed unusually large. Keep in mind that Lisa's hospital charged $350 per day and that only covered room and food. Everything else was listed as a "fee for service." This way the hospital was able to get more money either from the insurance companies or the patients themselves in out-of-pocket* *expenses. Other hospitals have a daily charge that covers everything.*

*The Watsons were looking over the extensive list of services billed to Lisa when they discovered a large number of discrepancies between the itemized statement submitted to the insurance company and Lisa's medical record.*

*One psychiatrist had billed for thirty-eight visits, yet the Watsons could find documentation for only fifteen. When they questioned Lisa, she told them that these fifteen visits were actually only brief stops on rounds that the psychiatrist made each morning. Every visit had occurred in the ward, without privacy, and lasted from three to five minutes. The doctor charged $55 for each of these visits. No matter how inadequate the Watsons viewed these fifteen visits from a therapeutic point of view, they had occurred and the insurance company paid for them.*

*The remaining twenty-three visits and other discrepancies the Watsons found in the bill added up to a 48 percent error rate. They challenged the bill and the hospital administration adjusted the bill in their favor.*

A difference of opinion between the hospital and you can come up at any time. One important record to resolve the differences is your child's medical record. If you claim that your child only got three visits, and the hospital claims twelve, you can check your child's medical record.

## Your Child's Medical Record

The Watsons were able to see Lisa's medical record because she had given permission for her parents to do so. The law varies from state to state as to who has access to the records of minors. You can check on your state by contacting your state Attorney General.

It is always proper to consider your child's preference about showing you her medical record, but since you have to be concerned with her long-term care, this is information you may need. The Watsons decided that they needed access to Lisa's records, got her permission, and then made an appointment with the hospital staff to examine the medical record at a specific time. It took them about an hour, but both parents were familiar with medical records – Bob is a dentist and

Donna a physical therapist. It may take you longer, or you may want to hire a consultant to work with you.

Be prepared to encounter resistance from the hospital staff when you tell them that you want to see your child's medical record. Most of them are not used to patients or their families exercising their rights. Psychiatric hospitals are big business, but they are not eager to view you as a consumer. They are more familiar with the philosophy that they "know best," and don't want to get involved in working with the family in these ways. Your lawyer should always be able to get access, providing your child gives her permission.

A possible exception to this is material in your child's *risk management file*. Some procedures are not documented in detail in the medical record and a subpoena may be required to gain access to the information in a risk management file.

> *This happened to Donna Watson. When Lisa came home on a short visit from the hospital, Donna noticed a scar on Lisa's right wrist. Lisa explained that she had become despondent after being involuntarily placed in a seclusion room for several days. She had not been allowed to talk to her parents or make any calls outside. She had felt helpless. She had cut her wrist with the jagged edge of a coke can. No one had notified her parents of her suicide attempt.*
>
> *The Watsons immediately confronted the hospital staff and asked why they had not been notified. When they requested to see the "incident form" describing the attempt, they were told that the form was not in the file and they would need a subpoena to view it.*

When the hospital staff thinks that they may have made a mistake of some sort and therefore be open to legal action, they often put the documentation on these events in their risk management file. This helps reduce the number of people who can see the report and act on it.

The Watsons' story is just one example of how important it is that you know as much as possible about this miniature world that is caring for your child. The most critical element in this world is the staff. These professionals are the ones who will diagnose your child, determine her treatment plan, and implement it. They are the ones who will prepare her for going home and becoming part of a larger world. You will be working with them and you need to know who they are and what they do.

All children in a psychiatric hospital, no matter what the illness, will come in contact with a variety of medical professionals. I have tried to list the most common ones, and the titles usually used for them. It is possible that the title may be slightly different from one hospital to another, but just ask what the professional's specific duties are.

## Members Of The Treatment Team

**Psychiatrists** are physicians which means that they have a medical degree (M.D.). Most psychiatrists have had a three year residency in psychiatry and child psychiatrists have specialized training in working with children and adolescents who have psychiatric disorders. Child psychiatrists have five years of specialized training. They prescribe medication as well as other forms of treatment for psychiatric disorders.

**Psychiatric Nurses** are licensed, professional, registered nurses who have expertise in psychiatric and mental health nursing. They will have the most day-to-day contact with your child and will supervise much of her care under orders from the physician as to what that care should be.

**Licensed Practical Nurses** have graduated from a formally approved program of practical nursing education and provide less intensive nursing services under the guidance of the psychiatric nurse.

**Mental Health Workers** have completed a formal course of study and are usually considered part of the nursing service department. Their duties vary according to the hospital but they generally provide services under the guidance of the psychiatric nurse.

**Psychologists** usually have a doctoral degree in psychology and will be involved in the therapy of your child. They do not prescribe medications, but will often be in charge of the psychotherapy approach chosen by your child's psychiatrist. They often assist in developing an atmosphere that fosters psychological growth on the ward. This is often referred to as *milieu therapy*.

**Social workers** provide social services to help you, your child, or others. They can help you with the various agencies involved in caring for your child, help you find social services, and act as your guide through the maze of paperwork.

**Family therapists** handle whatever family therapy your psychiatrist thinks your family needs. Family therapy as a treatment approach is covered more thoroughly in Chapter 1.

**Occupational therapists** are specially trained to evaluate your child's ability to work. These therapists plan and implement programs to help your child with her employment skills and leisure activities among other things.

**Recreational therapists** are trained to plan, implement, and evaluate recreational activities that take into account the special problems your child may have as a result of her mental illness.

**Child life workers** provide a variety of special services for your child depending on her needs. They help develop and implement therapeutic plans for your child including therapeutic play activities.

**Special education teachers** plan and implement a curriculum based on the special needs your child may have as a result of her mental illness.

# When It's Time To Consider Having Your Child Return Home

At some point in your child's treatment, you will probably have to plan for her return to active participation in your family. If she has been hospitalized, first she will be coming home for visits, then for longer and longer stays, until finally she may be able to live at home. Families look forward to their child coming home because it means progress in treatment. If she has never been hospitalized but has been in active therapy, then most of her emotional life has been spent in getting better. Now that she is making progress, it is time to plan for her becoming a fully participating member of the family again.

Most parents feel a little extra pressure to make their child feel welcome, wanted, and comfortable in this transition time. Sometimes, everyone wants so much to do well that they become more than eager; they become anxious. Often parents have never had to face incorporating their child back into the family after a psychiatric hospitalization or intensive treatment. You can overcome this lack of experience with a bit of careful planning.

## Plan

Working with the psychiatric team, you can plan ways to make your child's reentry process go as smoothly as possible. The most important thing to keep in mind is that the transition period can produce anxiety and tension for everyone. It is perfectly normal to feel unsure of yourself. If you anticipate problems, you can prepare for them. In fact, you can rehearse possible responses to different situations. Psychologists call this kind of advance preparation *anticipatory guidance*.

To help you remember the steps in this process, focus on the acronym P.L.A.N., which stands for Plan, Learn, Anticipate, and Negotiate. Plans should be based on the consensus of *both parents*. Consistent, well thought out approaches to managing the family, methods of discipline, and rules of conduct, including curfews should be clearly agreed on by the parents before they are discussed with the children. Knowing parental expectations and agreeing on ways to handle family tasks is important for all children, but it is *crucial* for children who have emotional problems. They *must* have predictability and structure in their lives.

## Learn

The first step in the planning process is to learn from the experts about your child's condition. You need to learn what her treatment consists of so that you will be able to help them evaluate how she is doing in the community. You may need to monitor her response to medication. Therefore, you need to be informed about the drug treatment prescribed. You need to learn from the team about how to manage behavioral problems that may occur as a result of the illness, the effects of any medication, or a combination of other factors.

*Lisa had been in a private psychiatric hospital for four months when her treatment team told the Watsons that they were considering having her go home for a short visit. She had had a rocky start to her hospitalization four months ago and they had all come a long way together since then.*

*When Lisa was first taken to this new hospital, her new team took her off her major tranquilizer to learn about her illness and consider possible ways to help her. It is normal to withdraw medication from patients and to observe them in a drug free state when the disorder is fairly recent. Professionals then make assessments and plan treatment. While off her medication, Lisa had a relapse.*

*After her relapse, Lisa was placed on high doses of Haldol, yet her symptoms persisted. Lisa was having a rough time. Her parents and sister were having an equally tough time because Lisa was not progressing. After leaving the first hospital, she got better. But she seemed so vulnerable, so fragile! The relapse was very hard on all the family because the progress she had made was now gone and Lisa was suffering again.*

*It took a lot of work over the next four months to get Lisa to the point where the staff, and the Watsons, could consider having her come home on a short pass. The staff had to make Lisa's stay in the hospital as nonstressful as possible. People with a fragile hold on reality need protection from stressful stimulation until they have learned ways to cope. They had to develop a stress management plan for Lisa that could be transferred to the outside world as she got passes. This would provide opportunities to try different plans with the support and guidance of the staff and the Watsons and see what worked best.*

## Anticipate

*Lisa was able to have short passes home even though she was not totally in remission from her illness. The psychiatrist had informed the Watsons that Lisa's attention span was presently at fifteen minutes. This meant that she could only pay attention to tasks for a maximum of fifteen minutes each. Structure was extremely important to Lisa since the staff had observed that if left to her own devices, Lisa would wander about the unit aimlessly. They had developed a list of activities for her to do all day and evening. The staff could refer Lisa back to the list of activities that was pinned to her desk when they noticed that she seemed confused. Making a list and referring her to it throughout the day appeared to help her perform better.*

*Next, the staff pointed out to Donna and David that their usual way of communicating with Lisa would need to change. Sentences that were too long or conveyed too many choices could result in more confusion and discomfort for Lisa. The staff em-*

*phasized the importance of using short, concrete terms in talking with Lisa. The psychiatrist had overheard Donna talking to Lisa while they were waiting to begin a four-hour pass.*

*"Well, Lisa, we are going to take you out for lunch. Where do you want to go?"*

*Lisa put her hand to her throat, backed away from her parents and stuttered, "I . . . I . . . I . . ."*

*Both David and Donna stared at Lisa and were visibly shaken.*

*Next time they met with the psychiatrist he told them that the statement was too vague and offered Lisa too many choices. He said they should never give her more than two choices. They might consider what her favorite foods are and then say, "Do you want a hamburger or a hot dog?"*

*It took a while for her parents to learn how to communicate with Lisa in this new, somewhat artificial manner. Eventually, the style of communication which was simpler, less vague, and briefer than their normal way of behaving became the norm for talking with Lisa. But it was at considerable psychological cost to her parents. This communication style did not allow for humor, satire, or much spontaneity. Lisa did not seem to "catch" the jokes or find them humorous. However, with time, practice, and coaching from the staff, the Watsons adapted to Lisa's illness.*

Because the particular needs of communicating with your child may be somewhat different than what the Watsons faced, talk with her therapists and learn about specific techniques for your situation. Again, that is why it is important to have a good working relationship with the professionals treating your child.

## Negotiate

*In planning for the pass from the hospital, the Watsons learned techniques for structuring Lisa's day. They anticipated hurdles and planned ways to address them. The night before Lisa was scheduled to go home, Donna set a time to meet with her at the hospital to plan the entire eight-hour pass. The nurse informed Donna that Lisa's attention span was still at fifteen minutes. Consequently, the plan included activities and events that could accommodate a schedule broken into fifteen-minute intervals. Lisa was still intellectually impaired and exhibited bouts of confusion, which meant that she needed help in knowing the time, date, and what was happening in the outside world. They planned activities that avoided overstimulation. As with all stress management plans, they needed to include time for fun activities and rest.*

*Lisa and Donna met in Lisa's room at the hospital and jointly developed a schedule. A time was established for picking her up and returning her to the hospital. Then the activity that Lisa wanted to accomplish most was identified. Lisa wanted to go to her favorite Italian restaurant. Lisa felt she could manage the lunch if it lasted no more than one hour. Donna said that she would make reservations for 1 P.M., since the rush might be over by then and there would be less noise and bustle. They planned a half hour each getting to and from the restaurant. Lisa decided to plan a forty-five-minute nap after the lunch. Donna told Lisa that many of her friends had called and wanted to see her. The staff had not allowed them to visit because Lisa had experienced many setbacks since entering the hospital. Lisa stated that seeing too many of them would be too stressful at this time. She needed time to figure out how to respond to them and she wasn't ready. However, she might like to go to a movie with her best friend, Mary. Donna negotiated with Lisa to wait on the movie. This was the first pass and she didn't want her to overdo things. Could she wait until a later time for that? Lisa reluctantly agreed to give up the idea of the movie, but wanted to visit Mary for a while. So a half hour was set aside for the visit. Lisa decided to walk to Mary's so that she could leave when she wanted to.*

## Schedule for Lisa's Eight-Hour Pass

*10:00*    *Pick up Lisa. Have guitar packed. Get medication. Sign out.*

*10:30*    *Arrive at home. See Sherlock the cat, play with him. Talk with Amy.*

*10:45*    *Call Mary and tell her that I'll drop by at 3:30. Straighten up desk.*

*11:00*    *Rest for 15 minutes.*

*11:15*    *Listen to David Bowie records in my room.*

*11:30*    *Do math homework.*

*11:45*    *Write in notebook. Start a short story.*

12:00    *Take medication.*
12:15    *Go for a walk with Mom.*
12:30    *Freshen up for lunch. Leave for the restaurant.*
1:00–2:00 *Eat lunch.*
2:00–2:30 *Drive home with Mom, Dad, and Amy.*
2:30–3:15 *Take nap.*
3:15–3:30 *Walk to Mary's house.*
3:30–4:00 *Visit with Mary.*
4:00–4:15 *Walk home from Mary's house.*
4:15–4:30 *Have a snack. Chocolate yogurt.*
4:30–4:45 *Ride bike.*
4:45–5:00 *Rest.*
5:00–5:15 *Listen to records.*
5:15–5:30 *Write short story in log.*
5:30–5:45 *Do English homework. Take medication.*
5:45–6:00 *Brush teeth and get ready for supper.*
6:00–6:30 *Eat dinner.*
6:30–7:00 *Wash dishes with Amy. I do dishes, Amy cleans table and sweeps kitchen.*
7:00–7:15 *Attend family meeting. Plan for next visit and tell what chores I want to do.*
7:15–7:30 *Watch TV News.*
7:30–8:00 *Go back to the hospital. Say goodbye.*

## Evaluating Lisa's Visit

*Lisa was instructed to cross off the activities that she completed. In this way she felt partially in control of her life. This bolstered her self-confidence and helped her add some predictability and success to her life. By talking about how the time passed and how she tolerated the events, the staff and the Watsons learned about adding or deleting items for the next time.*

*The family meeting that occurred toward the end of Lisa's first pass was used to develop a division of labor for the next week's visit. It became a weekly ritual to structure the next visit. All members knew when their tasks were to be completed and what was expected of them. The assignments were posted on the refrigerator. In addition, the members praised each other for jobs well done and offered suggestions. The weekly family meeting also provided information about how the behavior of each person affected others. For example, if Lisa completed the dishes on time, David pointed out that he was grateful to her because it allowed him more time to shop for groceries or to play cards with the family. Feedback to others was offered in the spirit of criticizing the behavior, not the person.*

## Positive Reinforcement

By recognizing Lisa's good performance in the assigned tasks, David was reinforcing it. By praising good behavior, the behavior is reinforced and more likely to occur in the future. Giving people silver stars, passes, money, citations, or the like are also methods of reinforcing positive actions. Some psychiatric facilities use variations of these methods to shape or change a person's behavior. This technique is referred to as *behavior modification*. To be effective, the behavior modification plan should be tailored to your child's particular needs.

A great deal of controversy exists about the use of these forms of behavior modification in psychiatric facilities. Token economy programs are variations on the behavior modification theme. Parents must learn how these "rewards" and "punishments" are applied to see if they seem reasonable for their child. Usually the hospital administration has copies of the policies used to apply these procedures. Ask to see them. You can use some of these techniques when your child comes home.

Use what you've learned about behavior modification at your family meetings to tell your child in advance what the rules are and how they will be enforced. For example, she can't drive the family car if the trash is not emptied by six o'clock each evening. In this manner you can help to shape her behavior positively. Be prepared for some uproar from your child, who may not want to change. After all, we all know how difficult it is to drop old habits and to develop new ones.

Both parents must agree on what the rules are in advance, and what the consequences will be if the child does not follow those rules. You must be firm. If your child senses that you can be made to back down on your demands by having a temper tantrum, then she will have several. Ignore them or leave or leave the room. Don't argue with her in the heat of the moment. Your actions speak for themselves and if she does not comply with the rules, follow through with the withdrawal of the privilege. When she does complete the activity, be sure to acknowledge and reward her efforts.

**Avoid Physical Punishment.** No matter what behavior patterns you want to change in your child, physical punishment is not the way to get that behavior. Studies have shown that your child will comply with your request as long as she is being physically punished, but the actions you want to change with the punishment will return when you are not around. She does not really learn new behavior patterns through punishment, she merely suppresses the urge until you are out of the picture.

In summary, avoid physical punishment and emphasize rewards for positive interchanges with others and jobs completed, because these actions tend to strengthen behavioral change. Rewards will vary with the particular interests of your child. Rewards can be warm, positive comments directed to your child about her performance or they can take the form of material objects, such as candy. Obviously, you have to consider the age of your child and her current level of functioning when deciding on the method of reward. As much as possible you want to appeal to her maturity level.

## Analyzing The Visit

*As a result of analyzing the results of the home visit and talking it over with the psychiatrist at the next meeting, the Watsons had to consider the difficulty Lisa had in managing too much stimulation. Because of her medication, she could not manage visually complex stimulation or tolerate sound levels that were loud or high pitched. Bright lights bothered her a great deal. Not only did these sensitivities limit her participation in common activities like driving in congested traffic, but they also put rock concerts, movies like* Star Wars, *and large parties with noise and strangers temporarily on hold.*

After each of your child's home visits, you will want to go over what happened with her team also. Your observations on how things went and how she responded will be very important when the team plans for the next step in her treatment.

## Becoming Adept Observers

Use what happens at home to learn how to manage different situations. Remember that this has to be done in a nonintrusive way. For instance, if your child gives you feedback that you are coming on too strong, meaning that your intentions are good but being around you too much is bothersome to her, then back off for a while. Withdrawal is a normal reaction to an overstimulating environment. It is her perception about these events that matters. Learn to listen to her talk and understand her feelings.

*With the knowledge that a too stimulating environment was disruptive to Lisa's fragile psychological balance, the Watsons made the following changes:*

1. *Since Donna was hard of hearing and Lisa complained about the loud volume of the television, they got Lisa ear plugs and Donna a hearing aid. It would have been possible to get Lisa a TV set for her room, but they had observed that she liked to be in the family room with them.*
2. *The Watsons were willing to turn off the lights in the family room when Lisa was present. Bright lights bothered her.*
3. *They got Lisa a special type of wrap-around sunglasses that reduced the brightness when she went outside.*
4. *They continued to make the written lists of activities with Lisa after her discharge for as long as she felt she needed to make them.*
5. *If Lisa appeared to be irritated with them, they tried to reduce contact with her. They did not do it in a rejecting or hostile manner. They merely recognized that this amount of personal contact upset her. Indicating to your child that it is all right to temporarily withdraw from stimulating events is a sign that you understand her stress level and is a step in the direction of coping with her illness.*

*The above schedule and analysis shows how Lisa's family applied the P.L.A.N. approach to her first home visit. The family members also informed the team about the goals they wanted to address. Donna anticipated potential problems and negotiated with Lisa on ways to manage the day. David and Donna had explained to the treatment team before Lisa was admitted that they needed to have access to the professionals treating their daughter. Therefore, when they had observations to make about Lisa's behavior, the staff was prepared to listen to them.*

Your child's professional team can learn from you too. You may want to complete the form in Appendix E called *The Evaluation of the Home Visit*. You respond to the questions on the form and give the treatment team at the hospital a copy of the results. This information can help them understand the real effects of their treatment plans.

## The Discharge Plan

Let's return to the Watsons and see how they were faring in their efforts to bring Lisa home nine months after the beginning of Lisa's illness.

*The physician believed that Lisa's condition was a* bipolar affective disorder *rather than schizophrenia. She was placed on lithium, a mood-regulating medication. Lisa was back again. She looked like the old Lisa, except she was heavier. She had the same goals as before—going to college, getting boyfriends, and buying clothes. She was almost normal. No, she was normal! Now that her diagnosis had been established, as long as she developed a stress management plan, took her medication, and was careful, she could go on with her life. The discharge plan developed by the team looked like this:*

1. *Lisa had completed high school while in the hospital. The diploma was granted from her original school rather than the special school at the hospital.*
2. *Lisa was to see a psychologist once a week.*
3. *She was to see a psychiatrist who would prescribe medication, monitor the effects, and treat her while she was attending college.*
4. *For the six-week period that occurred between release from the hospital and beginning college in January, she would work at a fast food restaurant.*
5. *During this six-week period, Lisa would see her psychologist.*
6. *Lisa would go away to a small, rural, liberal arts college. Lisa had wanted to attend a college two blocks from home. This item requires some background information.*

# Family/Staff Disagreements On Treatment And Discharge Plans

*The staff felt that Lisa should get away from her family. They viewed the Watsons as a highly emotional family. They did not understand the extreme distress or the grief that the Watsons were experiencing. In only a few months, their daughter and had gone from a popular, pretty actress to a withdrawn, hallucinating, and disordered person. In addition to coping with the catastrophic illness afflicting their daughter, they had to contend with the rude, inaccurate deductions about the cause of Lisa's illness made by those who were supposed to be helping them. They had to hire a lawyer to see that Lisa would remain out of seclusion and out of cold wet sheet packs, an old-fashioned device that the staff thought calmed her. Lisa viewed this as punishment and hated it. Lisa and her parents wanted her to leave as soon as she was stabilized. The staff wanted her to remain in the hospital for a year. The staff compromised and recommended attendance at college* away from home.

*Everything went smoothly for the Watsons until Lisa started college. Four days after school began, she had a relapse. She had been urged to try out for a play by her new roommate. The other girls in the dorm had encouraged her also. The group pressure resulted in her reading for the part and having a breakdown at that time. Peer pressure and beginning a full-time course of study during the middle of the normal academic year resulted in tremendous pressure. In retrospect, the crisis might have been avoided by having Lisa take only one course, or perhaps letting her audit a course at the college near her home.*

If you feel that the recommendations of the treatment team are not right for your child, follow your own instincts. You know your youngster better than anyone and you have to live with the consequences of the decisions you make.

As a final note about difficulties that arise between professionals in hospitals and families, it is possible for families to air their grievances with the administration. If further action is required, you can request interviews with surveyors of the Joint Commission on Accreditation of Health Care Organizations (JCAH) when they make the site visit to the hospital. The usual procedure is to inform the director of the hospital that such a public hearing is requested. Ask him to inform the staff at the JCAH headquarters in Chicago and ask that you be informed of the date of the survey. To ensure that communication is established, a carbon copy of the letter should be sent to the JCAH office with a cover letter requesting that they also inform you of the survey date. A sample letter and the address of the JCAH office is available in Appendix D.

# Extra Effort

Studies have shown that members of minority groups do not have the same access to mental health care as others. If you are a member of a minority group, you may need to be more aggressive in trying to get the care the health care system should provide your child. Consider contacting the local Mental Health Association or the Alliance for the Mentally Ill in your area for help. Your representative in Congress or the Senate may also be useful in that regard.

Many families and must go that extra mile in order to get the services their children need. The concept of "extras" is important in planning for reentering the world outside of the hospital.

*Lisa Watson taught her parents about extras during a weekend pass from the hospital.*

*It was two o'clock in the morning and Donna was asleep when there was a quiet tap, tap, tap at the bedroom door. Donna said, "Come in."*

*Lisa opened the door and said, "Mom, I need a little extra." She was wearing the blue and white striped oxford shirt that she used as a nightgown and black ballet slippers. She was rubbing her eyes.*

*Donna thought she wanted an extra tranquilizer, which she was entitled to if she couldn't sleep. "What do you mean, you want extra?"*

*Lisa put out her arm, sat on the edge of the bed and said softly, "Mom, it's too cold in my room and I need an extra hug. I need your advice. What shall I do?"*

*Donna said, "Well, come over here and I'll give you an extra hug. Then you can turn off the air conditioner and go back to sleep. What did you do at the hospital when you needed an extra?"*

*"Well, I asked for it, naturally. Jean taught me that if I needed extra medication, sleep, or love, just ask for it. She said I should ask for anything I needed to make it through the day. I would go up to the staff, just the special ones like Jean or Margaret, and ask them for a hug. They always gave it to me."*

## Conclusion

Being able to ask for "extras" is good preparation for reintroducing your child community living. If your child's needs are known you are more likely to get some of them met. Families are often the people who provide the "extras" for discharged patients. They often need "extras" too. We all need things; if you can learn to ask for them, you will probably get some of the ones you need and be better able to cope with life. The most important thing that you can do for your child is keep yourself as healthy as possible. She will need your strength to help her through this time and you will need extras, too, in order to make sure that she gets what she needs, both at home and in your community. It is not an easy job, but you can do it.

## REFERENCES

Anderson, C. M. et al. *Schizophrenia and the Family.* New York: Guilford Press, 1986.

Anthony, W. A. et al. "Psychiatric Rehabilitation." In *The Chronic Mental Patient: Five Years Later,* edited by John A. Talbott, 137–58. New York: Grune & Stratton, 1984.

Bernheim, Kayla F. and Anthony F. Lehman. *Working with Families of the Mentally Ill.* New York: W. W. Norton & Company, 1985.

Caplan, Gerald. *Principles of Preventive Psychiatry.* New York: Basic Books, 1964.

Gattozzi, Ruth. *What's Wrong with my Child?* New York: McGraw-Hill, 1986.

Harbin, H. "Family Treatment of the Psychiatric Patient." In *Psychiatric Hospital and the Family.* New York: SP Medical and Scientific Book, 1982.

Hatfield, A., ed. *Consumer Guide to Mental Health Services.* Arlington, VA: National Alliance for the Mentally Ill(1901 N. Fort Myer Drive, Suite 500, Arlington, VA 22209). 1985.

Kimble, G. A. *Hilgard and Marquis Conditioning and Learning.* East Norwalk, CT: Appleton-Century-Crofts, 1961.

Korpell, H. S. *How You Can Help: A Guide for Families of Psychiatric Hospital Patients.* Washington, D.C.: American Psychiatric Press, 1984.

Plotkin, R. "Limiting the Therapeutic Orgy: Mental Patients' Rights to Refuse Treatment." *Northwestern University Law Review* 72 (1977): 461–525.

Rutter, M. *Helping Troubled Children.* New York: Plenum Press, 1977.

Torrey, E. F. *Surviving Schizophrenia: A Family Manual.* New York: Harper and Row, 1983.

Walsh, M. *Schizophrenia: Straight Talk for Families and Friends.* New York: Wm. Morrow and

Company. 1985. Read chapter 8, "Parents as Psychovermin: Why You Are Being Blamed." Discusses the theoretical reasons professionals have used for blaming families.

Wynne, L.C. et al., eds. *Systems Consultation: A New Perspective for Family Therapy.* New York: Guilford Press. 1986.

Joint Commission on Accreditation of Hospitals (JCAH). *Accreditation Manual for Hospitals.* Chicago: JCAH, 1987.

# Parent Statements

Joan was well enough to have passes and later on was discharged. Our other daughter, Mary, was dethroned from her "only child," status which she had enjoyed immensely. All of a sudden she was thrust back into the "younger child" role. She got angry and took it out on us. We had developed a different family lifestyle while Joan was in the hospital and now everything she had gotten used to was changed. Again. We almost had more trouble with our Mary than Joan. At the time you never think of these things, but they sure become obvious later.

═❀═

While Ed was in the hospital, I functioned just fine. I know now that I was on auto pilot, but I seemed so in control. I marched from day to day doing all the things that needed to be done, but once he came home and I could see that he was really better, I collapsed. I cried for weeks, I shook a lot, couldn't work; I was a mess.

═❀═

The first hospitalization wasn't too bad, but once he had to go in again, we realized that this was ahead of us for the rest of our lives. Sometimes he's fine, and can work, then he starts getting strange and has to go back in. We just have so much pain realizing that our only child will be sick like this all his life.

═❀═

Our son never wants to invite his friends over when his sister is home on a pass. Janie has convulsions and serious behavioral

problems and Tim is afraid she'll have one of her famous temper
tantrums and embarrass him.

≡✹≡

Our daughter, Terry, was hospitalized in one of the state hospitals
for a month for psychiatric problems. She is manic depressive
and was driving recklessly and had an accident. Then she had
an argument with a cop and hit her. She went to jail and caused such a ruckus that the guards couldn't control her. Finally
she ended up in the state hospital and they could tell what was
really wrong with her. They got her calmed down and on medication. She's not perfect. Still strange, but we can reach her. She's
good enough to be home and get treatment from here.

≡✹≡

My ten-year-old son just got out of the hospital. He is 5'11" and
weighs 180 pounds. He's always getting in trouble. Last week
he started one of the city bulldozers that was parked across the
street and drove it away. He aimed it at an old lady in a
wheelchair. She got out just in time, but he flattened the chair.
He hit three cars and kept on going until he rammed a house.
Now he's in trouble with the law. I can't handle him. I'm afraid
of him so my husband has to stay home from work. I know we
need to find some place for him so he can get help. The hospital
says he doesn't need to stay there; that he can live at some kind
of special school but I need some help in finding a place.

≡✹≡

The doctors say Tammy has an organic condition. Whatever that
is! The social service department said that we would have to
give up custody before they would help. That means that we
aren't in charge of our daughter any more. It's like a punishment
or something. That's not right. Even if we do give them custody,
they said there weren't many places that would take her. Usually
they send kids like her out of state. The law's crazier than she
is. Because she's sick, they're going to take her away from us

and put her so far away that we'll have to take all day just to go see her.

We have another problem now. My mother is living with us and she doesn't understand Luke's illness and they really get on each other's nerves. She's tidy and neat and it drives her crazy to see Luke wandering around the house dropping things all over. His room looks like a mess. We just leave him alone, but she follows him around picking up after him and bugging him to pick up or clean up. He needs a lot more space than she'll give him. I wish there were some kind of program to teach her about his illness so maybe she'd just let him be.

One of the most insensitive things the therapist did was to videotape us and call us by name so anyone who saw the tape knew who we were. We thought that professionals would treat us in a dignified manner but they laughed at us and kept pointing out how typical we were of a schizophrenogenic family. We didn't even know what the term meant, but we did know what it meant to be laughed at.

Our daughter was always very smart. Her IQ was about 140. She was "normal" all her life, then suddenly she was a surly, angry sixteen-year-old. We couldn't leave her alone for more than an hour. We couldn't go on vacation, go to the movies, or anything. My wife had to quit her job just to make sure she didn't become destructive. We finally got her some therapy and things have quieted down a lot.

Kim only had to be hospitalized once. It was really only a babysitting deal. They kept her under observation for a few days, then sent her home and told us to find a therapist. They gave us a list and we picked blind from it. We had no idea what questions to ask, what kinds of therapies there were, anything. We just went along with whatever the "experts" told us. We're a lot smarter now and a lot poorer. We went through four therapists before we found one willing to explore a biological cause for Kim's problems. Sure enough, we got her on medicine and all of a sudden a calm, rational, fun child emerged. She still has problems, but now she's free to work on them.

=✻=

Try telling someone your child just got out of a mental hospital. See how fast they back away, change the subject, and disappear.

=✻=

The hardest thing about Joe being in the hospital was that he lost any confidence he had that he was a worthwhile human being. I had to keep telling him how great he is, but sometimes I didn't really feel that way. I got angry that this was happening and I wanted to shake him and tell him to quit acting so weird. That's the trouble with a mental illness, you can't see what's wrong, so it isn't as real. You keep thinking it can be cured with a little will power. I had to go into therapy right along with Joe when he came home and now we both see his illness differently. He's able to run the house for me while I work. He feels good about it, and is even talking about taking a college course or two.

=✻=

FIVE

# The Legal Provisions for Your Child's Education

## PAUL McELROY, PH.D.

You have to know what your child is legally entitled to in an education before beginning the lengthy process of developing the right educational plan for him. Too often children have been shunted aside, and denied their right to an education because their parents didn't know what their rights were under the law. You can't assume that the educational authorities will tell you. Sometimes they just want to avoid the expense of a special education program for your child. Currently, three federal laws—the Education for All Handicapped Children Act (EHC), the Rehabilitation Act (RA), and the Protection and Advocacy for Mentally Ill Individuals Act of 1986—offer most of the provisions for education and protection of the mentally ill.

Following a brief review of the history of the education of the mentally ill, we will explore the provisions of federal and state education laws for the mentally ill, discuss recent court rulings regarding the implementation of these laws, and conclude by providing a brief guide to help you take advantage of these legal entitlements and the parents' rights created by them.

## A Brief History Of The Education Of The Mentally Ill In The U.S.

The treatment of the mentally ill in the United States has been a dismal chapter in the history of one of the most progressive nations on earth. Prior to the nineteenth century, virtually no provisions were made for the care of the mentally ill. Families would hide those who were afflicted. The mentally ill who left their families or were abandoned by them wandered the countryside until they came into conflict with the law and were imprisoned or placed in almshouses. The nature of mental illness was so poorly understood that references to demonic possession as an explanation were common.

By the middle of the nineteenth century, medicine had made some progress in identifying and defining mental illness. However, the response of society to the problem of mental illness was the development of asylums designed primarily to protect the public by isolating the mentally ill. The concept of providing education for the residents of mental asylums simply did not occur to the physicians and staff of these asylums.

During the twentieth century, treatment of the mentally ill improved somewhat and education was included as part of the rehabilitation efforts. The advent of psychotropic drugs made treatment, education, and rehabilitation more feasible. The better private institutions began to include schools for their younger mentally ill patients and modest rehabilitation services for all patients. Treatment in the majority of publicly funded institutions, however, continued to be scandalously ineffective and efforts at education were equally feeble through the 1940s. Further, it was quite difficult to have someone committed to a public institution unless he had committed a dangerous crime or become a source of public embarrassment. The public institutions were among the worst facilities in the country and functioned as little more than badly run prisons.

In the late 1950s, a series of revelations by newspapers and magazines exposed the sorry state of affairs in mental institutions. The response was a movement called *deinstitutionalization* which resulted in the permanent closure of many of the public and some of the private institutions. Although community-based, part-time facilities were supposed to be made available for patients who had been left without care following deinstitutionalization, many mental patients were turned out into the streets due to lack of funds and the unresponsiveness of the public and public officials. Under these circumstances, education and rehabilitation efforts were reduced to an even greater extent than was treatment and housing.

The Supreme Court decision in *Brown v. Board of Education* in 1954 established the concept that education was critical to society and that to be excluded from an education was to be cut off from meaningful participation in that society. Although the case dealt specifically with the exclusion of Blacks from the public schools, the case demonstrated that education was essential for the equal treatment of any minority, including the handicapped. The decision stimulated the advocates of the handicapped to create change in the education of the handicapped by utilizing the courts.

By 1970, of an estimated four million seriously mentally ill persons, less than 800,000 or 20 percent were receiving adequate treatment. Of the one million school-age children in this group, less than 25 percent were receiving an appropriate form of education. Most state legislatures had incorporated provisions into their constitutions that established a legal basis for the systematic exclusion of the handicapped, including the mentally ill, from education. The statutes usually stated that "children of school age who are unable to benefit from education because of severe mental or physical handicaps are not required to attend the public schools." The justification for these provisions was that the handicapped were unable to profit from education and damaged the morale of the other school children. It was in this climate of public opinion that parents and other friends of the handicapped began to work to establish a free and appropriate system of education for handicapped children.

In 1971 a landmark decision by a federal district court held that the total exclusion of mentally retarded children from the Pennsylvania school system violated the U.S. Constitution. The court ruled that the school system must provide retarded children a hearing before they can be denied a public education. The school system had contended that the severely retarded could not benefit from schooling and that they therefore did not fall into the class of persons who could be taught. The court concluded that "all mentally retarded persons are capable of benefitting from a program of education and training . . ."

In 1971 all handicapped persons, including the mentally ill, joined together in a suit against the District of Columbia. The District of Columbia had excluded all severely handicapped children from its school system. The court ruled that such an exclusion denied the handicapped an equal educational opportunity. The school system had attempted to defend the exclusions by citing the administrative problems and financial expense involved in holding hearings, establishing educational programs, and periodically reviewing placements. The court ruled that financial problems could not be used as an excuse to deny the interests and needs of the children. In the court's opinion, the need of the handicapped for an education was as great or greater than the need of the nonhandicapped.

These two decisions stirred the public to demand educational rights for the handicapped, including the mentally ill. Several groups began to lobby the U.S. Congress for legislation which would spell out in detail the specific rights of the handicapped to education and would include protection for these rights. Among the most prominent groups lobbying for this legislation were the National Association for Retarded Citizens and the Council for Exceptional Children. The law which they lobbied for and which was finally passed in 1975 was the Education for All Handicapped Children Act (EHC). The next section addresses the provisions of this act.

## Basic Provisions Of The Education For All Handicapped Children Act

The Education for All Handicapped Children Act (EHC) is a very extensive legislative action which extends educational entitlements to all handicapped children from the ages of three to twenty-one and includes detailed protection and safeguards to assure that the provisions are accorded fairly and equally. The term "handicapped children" is defined in the act to include the seriously emotionally disturbed. The term "seriously emotionally disturbed" is defined as follows:

The term means a condition exhibiting one or more of the following characteristics over a long period of time and to a marked degree, which adversely affects educational performance:
A. An inability to learn which cannot be explained by intellectual, sensory, or other health factors;
B. An inability to build or maintain satisfactory interpersonal relationships with peers and teachers;
C. Inappropriate types of behavior or feelings under normal circumstances;
D. A general pervasive mood of unhappiness or depression;
E. A tendency to develop physical symptoms or fears associated with personal or school problems.

The term includes children who are schizophrenic. The term does not include children who are socially maladjusted, unless it is determined that they are seriously emotionally disturbed.

In practical terms the definition means that to qualify as seriously emotionally disturbed under EHC the child must have a long-term emotional condition (generally the time period is six months or longer) with one of the characteristics listed or be diagnosed as schizophrenic. The conditions must be present to a marked degree and the emotional condition must adversely affect the child's educational performance. Clearly, the intent of the law as revealed by the definition of seriously emotionally disturbed is to limit the provisions only to those children who have been quite ill for an extended period of time. The law is also intended not to apply to children whose problems involve misbehavior rather than mental illness.

Unfortunately, schizophrenia is the only mental condition expressly identified as qualifying as a serious emotional disturbance. If your physician diagnoses your child as schizophrenic and his condition persists to a marked degree for more than six months, during which time his education is adversely affected, then your child qualifies for the provisions of the EHC. If your child has another mental illness, you will need to get a ruling on his eligibility from the school system.

Under the EHC, the Admissions, Review and Dismissal (ARD) team at the school where your child's special education is provided will design an educational plan for him by drawing up an *Individualized Education Plan* (IEP). The team includes a special education teacher, diagnostic personnel, you, and, where appropriate, your child.

The IEP includes an assessment of your child, a list of short term and annual goals, the specific educational services he will get, the date when he will start receiving these services, and a procedure for evaluating his progress.

These services must be provided in the *least restrictive environment* (LRE). The least restrictive environment is the school setting most like that for a normal student in which your child can still benefit from education. In practice this has encouraged the process popularly called *mainstreaming* in which the handicapped child is placed in a regular school and in typical classes or, if required, in regular classes for most subjects and in a special class within the school for special services that may be required by the handicap. This means that your child can stay in his community school, be with his friends, and not have to face the turmoil of changing his environment at a time when he needs to work on getting better.

For some severely and profoundly handicapped children, the least restrictive environment may be a special school or even a special institution providing around- the-clock treatment. State school systems have provided special schools for the handicapped. However, in some instances, the handicap may require residential placement. This is often true for the seriously mentally ill. Residential placements can cost as much as $200,000 a year. States and local systems of education have been extremely reluctant to provide these services to the mentally ill. A later section deals with this problem.

Under the EHC, your child must receive a *free appropriate public education* (FAPE). This includes related services which are needed so that he can benefit from education. The term *related services* includes transportation, supportive services, psychological services, physical and occupational therapy, and medical and counselling services. It also includes the early identification and assessment of your child's handicapping condition. This means that there are a wide variety of services to which your child is entitled. Be sure to ask exactly what these services are and how you can get them for your child.

There has been much controversy regarding the provision of psychological services through the EHC. Parents have argued that school systems should pay for the psychological services required by their mentally ill children to benefit from education including care in residential facilities. School systems have argued that the medical care and psychological services can be separated from the educational needs in most instances and that these noneducational services should be provided by the social service department. The result in most states has been a failure to accept responsibility for the education of the most severely mentally ill. This has been especially true in those cases where a special school for the handicapped is not adequate and residential treatment is needed.

The school systems in many states have also argued that psychotherapy and residential care are medical services and that these are specifically limited by the law to diagnostic and evaluative functions. Parents have filed many court suits requesting residential placement and related services with different outcomes in different areas.

The failure of many school systems to provide adequate related services and necessary treatment for all eligible students is a violation of the intent of the act. The inclusion in the act of the term "psychological services" in addition to medical services shows an intention of Congress to specifically require psychological support for mentally ill children. The EHC should be amended to specifically identify the school system as the agency responsible for providing adequate education and other related services when required for the child. Such a change would make one governmental agency responsible for all aspects of the education of the child and would correct the confusion that currently exists over which agency is to provide related services and residential placements.

# Parents' Rights Under The Education For All Handicapped Children Act

The EHC provides you, as parents of handicapped children, with an extensive variety of rights and procedures to protect those rights. In this section we will discuss your rights in the development of an IEP and your right to protest an IEP if you disagree with its recommendations.

### Parents' Rights with Regard to the IEP

The school system is required to screen for children with handicapping conditions that may hinder their ability to learn. If your child has a special education need, he will be assessed for what those needs are, and he will get an individualized education plan (IEP) designed to fulfill those needs. You must be notified of the plans for an assessment and of the results of that assessment. The following procedures are available to assure you of your rights under the EHC:

1. Your school district agency should give you notice in writing that an assessment of your child will be conducted. If this notice is not provided, you should immediately request a conference with school authorities.
2. The results of the assessment should be made available to you in writing. You have the right to examine all relevant records with respect to the identification, evaluation, and educational

placement of your child and to obtain an independent evaluation of him.

3. Your school district must provide written notice to you whenever it proposes to initiate a change in the IEP or refuses to initiate a change in the IEP when you have requested it.

4. The school district must provide an opportunity for you to present complaints with respect to any matter relating to the identification, evaluation, or educational placement of your child.

5. Whenever a complaint has been received regarding the identification, evaluation, or educational placement of your child, you have an opportunity for an impartial due process hearing.

6. You have the right to be represented by legal counsel and to have other professional assistance. Due to a recent amendment of the EHC, if you are successful in an administrative or judicial proceeding under the EHC, you can have your attorney's fees paid for you if the court so indicates.

If you disagree with the evaluation of your child, believing that it does not meet his needs, that your views were not fairly presented, or that the services provided are not permitting him to progress adequately, *disagree in writing*. Request an opportunity to meet with the local school officials and attempt to settle the problem at that level. Settlement at the level of the local school or agency is the simplest procedure and avoids the complications of further action.

If the local school or agency officials are uncooperative or unresponsive, it may be necessary for you to contact the superiors of the local agency to obtain cooperation. Usually this must take the form of a hearing before a neutral hearing official at which you and the superintendent's office are adversaries. In general, the courts require that administrative remedies be exhausted before a court case, injunction, or other legal action may be granted. Then you should meet with the superintendent or his designated representative before going to the hearing. When it becomes necessary to have a hearing with the central office of the school system, it is advisable for you to retain legal counsel and to obtain all of your child's school records. Parents are entitled to copies of all their child's school records. These must be made available to you before you take any legal action. Legal aid is sometimes available through community and parent advocates or legal services attorneys. The EHC does *not* provide attorneys' fees for the counsel of a lawyer who represents you before the superintendent's office.

## The Hearing Process

The first step in obtaining a hearing is to inform the local school officials and the state director of special education in writing that you are requesting a hearing to review your child's placement. State clearly why you believe the placement is incorrect or inadequate and briefly indicate objective, factual reasons for the problem. Provide the names of the persons involved in the decision and the dates of the decision. Also provide a chronology of your meetings with the local school officials, including the times, places, dates, persons, things discussed, and conclusions reached. An attorney's assistance in preparing the letter is essential. Send the letter by registered mail and keep a copy for yourself and your attorney. The school system must complete a hearing within forty-five days from the time the parents' letter is received.

Your hearing will be presided over by a hearing officer. The hearing officer must be impartial. He must not work for the school system or the agency dealing with your child and must not be involved with education in such a way as to conflict with the professional judgement required to make an impartial decision.

At the hearing you must be able to prove in a clear and convincing fashion that the school's approach to your child's education is inappropriate. You must present logical reasoning and the evidence of experts to win the hearing. Several good books have been written on the subject of special education hearings. Some of these books have been written for the legal counsel of school systems, providing detailed sets of questions to be asked of the parents and the parents' witnesses in order to win the hearing for the school system.

One book which presents excellent advice on how the school system can win a hearing is *The Easy Way to Win Special Education Hearings,* by Jane E. Slenkovich (Kingshorn Press, Inc., Stevens Creek Boulevard, Cupertino, CA 95014, 1982). This book presents information on such topics as preparing evidence, witnesses, outside experts, and detailed sets of questions for the school system's defense attorney. This volume is essential reading for you if you are to prepare an adequate presentation.

There are some further points regarding the hearing that you should consider. You have the right to bring anyone to the hearing, including lawyers, community advocates, special education professionals, testing experts, or independent evaluators. You may also wish to obtain an independent evaluation of your child's problem through a private agency. This can sometimes be very helpful in a hearing. However, you must pay for the independent evaluation unless a court determines that the evaluation should be paid for by the school.

You can *require* school officials to attend the hearing and either you or your attorney can question them. Your child can be present. Finally, and very importantly, you can prevent the school system from presenting any evidence that was not made available five days prior to the hearing. Of course, you must make all evidence presented by your advocates available five days prior to the hearing.

## Other Courses of Action

Another course of action is to complain to the Federal Office for Civil Rights in your district. They can also intercede on your behalf. This step may be advisable if meetings with the local school or agency are unsatisfactory and you anticipate problems in meeting with local school district officials. The local Office for Civil Rights may be able to give you good advice as you plan for further action.

The final step is an injunction and/or a lawsuit. This is generally the most expensive and time-consuming approach to the problem, but it is also often the only way to address the problem satisfactorily. At this point the advice of a competent attorney is essential. Because of the specialized nature of the law in the field of developmental disabilities and handicapping conditions, you need to be represented by attorneys who have made a specialty of this type of law.

Courts have the right to award reasonable attorney fees and costs to parents or guardians who win a court judgement. Parents who do not succeed in winning a court judgement are not eligible to be awarded either attorneys' fees or court costs. Therefore, you should either be prepared to pay the attorneys yourselves or make arrangements with a free legal aid service in your state. The Children's Defense Fund at 122 C Street, N.W., Washington, DC 20001, 202/628-8787 and 800/424-9602 publishes an excellent booklet with sources for legal aid in each state, which is available for $4.75 plus shipping and handling.

## Parents' Rights To Residential Placement And Related Services Under The EHC

There is great debate as to whether or not the EHC requires the school system to provide children with a residential placement and other related services as they need them. The school systems want to avoid the financial burden while parents want the best possible care for their children. In general, school systems have argued that residential placement is medical treatment not required by the EHC and that as noneducational care it should be the responsibility of rehabilitation or welfare agencies. On the other hand, parents have argued that residential placement involves psychological services which are identified separately from medical services in the EHC as being a form of related services available to handicapped children. Parents have pointed out that often the psychological, medical, and educational needs of the mentally ill are so interrelated as to be inseparable. Parents believe that the educational system must address all of these needs when concerned with education.

To date, the Supreme Court has yet to address a case which decides these issues clearly. Lower courts have issued decisions which are contradictory. The language of the EHC has not been clarified to settle the issue. Thus, the decision regarding residential placement at the expense of the school system varies with the state and the local system.

## The Rehabilitation Act

The Rehabilitation Act of 1973 provides a vast array of services at the state and local level. The intention is to assist both mentally and physically handicapped persons to be employed. As your child gets older and finishes school, this law will become more and more important to his future. It is a good idea to become familiar with it now.

The act can provide funds for the rehabilitation of mentally ill children, adolescents, and adults to assist them in preparing for the world of work through full-time, part-time, or transitional employment. The act was amended in 1986 to make it more easily applicable to the mentally ill.

One of the problems with the vocational rehabilitation program for persons who were being treated for mental illness was the fact that they were often considered unemployable because they could only tolerate transitional or part-time employment. Now part-time employment is specifically included and the definition includes supportive/transitional employment. Such a change of definition makes the act more useful in rehabilitating the mentally ill who may need part-time or transitional employment as part of their treatment or as a necessary preliminary to full-time employment.

The concepts of *supported employment* and *transitional employment* programs are also specifically included in the act under the new revisions. Supported employment is work that will further the employee's treatment and transitional employment is work that will help the employee move from a job that is designed around his therapy to more customary types of employment. These concepts recognize the need for support services for individuals with chronic mental illness in order for them to benefit from such programs. This will ensure that the vocational rehabilitation program can supply services that will be responsive to their needs.

The amendments also include an *individualized written rehabilitation program* (IWRP) which has been derived from the IEP concept. IWRPs are designed to provide people with mental illness with a plan specifically tailored to the needs of that person. Each IWRP must:

1. be developed to achieve vocational objectives;
2. include a statement of the long- range rehabilitation goals;
3. include a statement of the intermediate rehabilitation objectives;
4. where appropriate, include a statement of the specific services to be provided;
5. include an assessment of the expected need for post-employment services;
6. include a statement of the specific services to be provided and the projected dates for the initiation and the anticipated duration of each service;
7. include objective criteria and an evaluation procedure and schedule for determining whether goals and objectives are being attained;
8. provide for a reassessment of the need for post-employment services.

The IWRP must be reviewed at least once annually with the parent or the individual. The IWRP provides a way for you to make sure that your child is getting the vocational training he needs to become part of the work force. It also gives you an outline to chart his progress and see if his needs are being met.

## The Protection And Advocacy For Mentally Ill Individuals Act Of 1986

The Protection and Advocacy for Mentally Ill Individuals Act of 1986 provides protection and advocacy systems for the mentally ill. It is not specifically intended to provide education, but its provisions have some educational implications. The bill is of great importance to the mentally ill and has been included here because of this importance.

The legislation includes a statement by the Congress that mentally ill individuals are particularly vulnerable to abuse and that state systems for seeing that this abuse does not occur vary widely and are frequently inadequate.

The legislation is designed to ensure the protection of the rights of the mentally ill, provide advocates for them, ensure the enforcement of the federal and state statutes, and investigate incidents of abuse and neglect of mentally ill individuals. Abuse is defined to include sexual assault, the use of excessive force when placing a mentally ill individual into bodily restraints, and the use of bodily or chemical restraints in a manner that is not consistent with federal and state laws and regulations. The term "neglect" includes acts of omission such as failure to establish or carry out an appropriate individual treatment plan for a mentally ill individual or the failure to adequately provide for his physical needs and bodily safety.

The legislation has implications for the education of the mentally ill because a violation of a treatment plan can be considered neglect. If education is a part of the treatment plan of a mentally ill individual, then violation of the educational aspects of the treatment plan may constitute neglect and initiate the protection and advocacy provisions. These provisions provide funds for outside agencies to act as advocates. These advocates have access to records, the right to ask for administrative remedies, and the right to file suit if the administrative remedies are exhausted.

Many private, voluntary organizations such as the Alliance for the Mentally Ill, should be able to qualify under this act as advocacy and protection agencies. Regulations for the legislation as currently stated are still being developed. However, the need for such legislation should be obvious to anyone who has interacted with treatment agencies for the mentally ill on a long-term basis.

Title II of the act is called the Restatement of the Bill of Rights for Mental Health Patients. This title includes a detailed list of rights of mental patients. These rights are to be stated in language which is understandable to the persons to whom the rights are addressed and to be posted in appropriate locations. If you don't see it posted in your child's facility, ask to see a copy and then request that it be posted.

## Conclusion

As we can see from this chapter, we have come a long way from those early dark days when the mentally ill were shunted aside and ignored by society. Considerable progress has been made in establishing that persons with mental illness have rights and that a right to an education is included among those general rights. Today your child has a right to an education which includes related services and may also include residential placement. Your child also has a right to rehabilitation which includes supported and transitional employment programs.

Despite this record of progress, more needs to be done. The following brief set of recommendations highlights some of the needs not yet filled by the mental health system in the area of educational opportunities:

1. The local education agency must be designated as the agency responsible for providing and financing a free and appropriate education for school-age children. This is necessary to avoid the shuffling of mentally ill children between various public agencies each of which denies its own responsibility.
2. Federal funds should be provided to the states for allocation to the local education agencies to meet the obligations for the education of the mentally ill student.
3. Federal and state funding is needed for the education of mentally ill children and adults who have received an inadequate education because of the severity of their illness during the

period in their lives when they would qualify for education under Public Law 94–142.

4. Federal legislation is needed to clarify the mentally ill person's right to related services and residential treatment. Federal legislation needs to specify that, in the case of severely mentally ill individuals in need of residential placement, the educational, medical, and therapy needs are so intertwined that all three forms of treatment must be considered part of a single treatment plan and must be available to all severely mentally ill individuals. Such treatment must be provided and financed under the legal provisions addressed in recommendations (1) and (2) above.

It is good to know that our children can benefit under these new acts and as we move ever closer toward improved services for persons with mental illness, the picture becomes even brighter.

## REFERENCES

Brant, Jonathon. "Constitutional rights–patient rights–refusal of medication," 69 *Massachusetts Law Review* 98, June, 1984.

Hakola, Stewart R. "Attorney fees for representing persons with disabilities: 1986 Handicapped Children's Protection Act," 66 *Michigan Bar Journal* 36–38, January, 1987.

Jones, Phillip R. *A Practical Guide to Special Education Law: Understanding and Implementation of 94–142.* New York: Holt, Rinehart & Winston, 1986.

Larson, David A. "What disabilities are protected under the rehabilitation act of 1973?" 16 *Memphis Law Review* 229, 1986.

Lentz, Susan S. "Policy in the guise of law: civil rights and mental illness," 28 *The Bench and Bar of Minnesota* 21–24, February, 1987.

Mane, Joseph. "Protection and advocacy extends to the mentally ill," 20 *Clearinghouse Review* 321, July, 1986.

Mattison, Deborah A. "Guardianship for persons with developmental disabilities," 66 *Michigan Bar Journal* 18, January, 1987.

Mitchell, Joyce Slayton. *Taking On The World: Empowering Strategies For Parents Of Children With Disabilities.* New York: Harcourt, Brace & Jovanovich, 1982.

Mort, Geoffrey. "Establishing a right to shelter for the homeless," 50 *Brooklyn Law Review* 939–994, Summer 1984.

O'Boyle, Robert M. "Voluntary minor mental patients: a realistic balancing of the competing interests of parent, child and state," 37 *Southwestern Law Journal* 1179, 1984.

"Parents desire for residential services and mainstreaming requirements in conflict," 7 *Mental and Physical Disabilities Law Reporter* 234–237, May–June, 1983.

Pullin, Diane. "Rights of students in need of special education," 66 *Michigan Bar Journal* 30–35, January, 1987.

"Rights in treatment/habilitation settings," 10 *Mental and Physical Disabilities Law Reporter* 283, July–August, 1986.

Rubenstein, Leonard S. "Access to treatment and rehabilitation for severely mentally ill poor people," 20 *Clearinghouse Review* 382–391, Summer 1986.

Schervish, Michael. "Rights of students in need of special education," 66 *Michigan Bar Journal* 17–32, January, 1987.

Schoenfeld, Benjamin N. "Civil rights for the handicapped under the Constitution and Section 504 of the rehabilitation act" 49 *Cincinnat Law Review* 580–610, 1980.
Shrybman, James A. *Due Process In Special Education.* Rockville, MD: Aspen Systems Corporation, 1982.
Slenkovich, Jane E. *The Easy Way To Win Special Education Hearings.* Cupertina, CA: Kingshorn Press, Inc., 1982.

CASE LAW

*Brown v. The Board of Education of Topeka, Kansas,* 347 U.S. 488, 1954.
*Mills v. The Board of Education of the District of Columbia,* 348 F. Supp. 866 (D.D.C. 1972).
*Pennsylvania Association for Retarded Children v. Commonwealth,* 344 F. Supp. 1257 (E.D. Pa. 1971), 343 F. Supp. 279 (E.D. Pa. 1972).

LEGISLATION

Education for All Handicapped Children Act, 20 USCA 1401, 1975.
Family Education Rights and Privacy Act (Buckley Amendment) 20 USCA 1232g (Cum. Supp. 1976).
Handicapped Children's Protection Act, Public Law 99–372, amending 20 USC 1415, effective August 5, 1986.
Protection and Advocacy for Mentally Ill Individuals Act of 1986 (Public Law 99–319) 42 USC 10801, 1986.
Rehabilitation Act Public Law 93–112, 87 Stat. 355, 1973.
Rehabilitation Act Amendments Public Law 99–506, 100 Stat. 1807, 1986.

# Parent Statements

We didn't have medical insurance to cover the extensive out-of-home treatment recommended for our daughter. Her doctor said that she needed special treatment and schooling in a place with experts to care for her.

George had to go to a boarding school for young children in a neighboring state. There isn't a school for him here where we live. We applied to the local school system to pay for the cost of this school and we're still waiting to hear from them. It's been months. If they don't pay, I don't know what we'll do. So far, we've taken out a second mortgage and my husband has a second job. Of course our savings went long ago to pay for our son's therapy.

The school told me that Joe is going to graduate from his residential treatment facility. The ARD (Admissions, Review and Dismissal Committee) discovered he has enough credits for his high school diploma so they have to graduate him, even though they don't think he's ready to leave emotionally. We can't afford to keep him there. His treatment is paid for by the school system but now they've found a way to push him out and get rid of him. Never mind that he still needs help. Legally, they have a way not to have to pay. It's so unfair.

=❀=

Julie is eighteen and diagnosed as manic-depressive. Her psychiatrist worked and worked to finally get her linked up with the vocational rehabilitation people. It always seems so difficult to get anything done.

=❀=

The counselor at school and the psychiatrist were great! They helped get tutors for her, so that she didn't fall too far behind. She managed to finish high school. Her grades weren't great, but she finished. They even managed to get her into a small college so she could study to be a teacher. They insisted on a small school so she would get individual attention and not be treated like a number. It's working out just fine.

=❀=

Things got so bad that Steven just quit. He was sixteen so he was legally able to drop out of school. It didn't matter that he was depressed and not able to make an intelligent decision, he quit and the school was only too glad to get rid of him. Now he doesn't do anything. He's given up on everything. There should be some way to make the school more supportive and not just lose kids like this.

=❀=

Alice's teacher didn't try to hide that Alice had problems. She made the whole class accept it as just a fact of life. Alice went off to her special education classes in the afternoon and there was no problem. When Alice forgot to take her medicine, the teacher would remind her. It was such a change to have someone so accepting. Alice just blossomed and now she even has a different attitude about her illness. She's not ashamed any more.

SIX

# Educational Services

PAUL D. McELROY, PH.D.

Everyone benefits from an education, including people with mental illness. There are a variety of educational services available to assist your child in obtaining the maximum benefit possible from her education. In this chapter, we will review these types of services. Then you can evaluate and select the type best suited to her needs. We will cover the importance of education for the seriously mentally ill, educational services and approaches, the characteristics of students with mental illness, the desirable characteristics of teachers of these students, and the need for additional programs for people who have recovered from mental illness.

## The Importance Of Education For The Mentally Ill

Education is critically important for the mentally ill, just as it is of critical importance for all individuals in our technologically advanced society. Unfortunately, parents and educators often put education aside because the mentally ill are not easily educated and require assistance in coping with the normal problems of living. In many cases, education is part of a child's overall treatment plan.

Although mental illness disrupts the educational process, this disruption can be minimized. The primary goal of any educational system for the mentally ill is to give them an education as close as possible to that of students without any handicapping condition. Mental illness must be dealt with in such a way that educational progress is as normal as possible.

One of the persistent myths concerning mental illness is that a person who becomes mentally ill remains mentally ill and is never able to function effectively in life. According to this line of reasoning there is no point in educating the mentally ill in a meaningful way because they will be unable to use the education provided. This is totally incorrect and the myth is so persistent that it must be specifically discredited. Approximately 80 percent of individuals afflicted with severe bipolar disorder can resume normal functioning for extended periods of time (two to twenty years). Among people diagnosed as schizophrenic about one-third recover completely, about one-third recover partially, and about one-third continue to suffer the illness in varying degrees. There is every reason for you to hope that your child can get better and rejoin your family and community as a fully functioning member.

This myth has been perpetuated by professionals who lose track of patients who recover and no longer seek therapy. Current research has established that over 70 percent of persons afflicted with severe depression are able to function effectively ten years later. These high rates of return to effective functioning even in the case of the most severe forms of mental illness emphasize the need to educate all mentally ill persons as thoroughly as possible so that they can contribute to society.

The statistics are in your favor. Your child has a good chance of recovering from her illness. Since you have every reason to hope for a good outcome, you should make sure that she continues her education to whatever degree possible. This means that she needs a special educational plan developed for her. The first step in drawing up this plan is to assess what she needs educationally and determine what her strengths are.

## Assessment

The team of individuals concerned with your child's education reviews all the assessment data. This team is called the ARD or Admissions, Review and Dismissal Team. It is one of the mandates of Public Law 94–142. The team normally consists of at least one of your child's teachers who is very familiar with her education, a representative of the health-care team, you, a special education teacher, and a representative of the school administration (either a principal, assistant principal, social worker, or counselor). Other persons may be members of the team. You have a right to attend the meeting and to be consulted in the determination of the time and place of the meeting of the ARD committee.

The team, after reviewing the data, will recommend whether or not your child can continue to attend her regular school. If she can, they will suggest the proper placement within the school. If not, then they will recommend a special school placement. In other words, they will be recommending the level of schooling they think appropriate for your child.

## Levels Of Schooling Available

Educational facilities for handicapped persons, including the seriously emotionally disturbed, are classified according to six levels, depending on how serious the problem is.

**Level I** involves the placement of the handicapped child in the regular classroom, but a special educational program is included for the child and special education consultants are available to the classroom teacher.

**Level II** involves placement of the child for most of the day in the regular classroom with attendance in special education classes or other special services in the school building for no more than one hour per day.

**Level III** is designed for a child who requires more extensive special education. The Level III child spends no more than an average of three hours per day in the special education classroom in a regular school or receiving special services in the general education classroom or in some other center in the regular school. The remainder of the day is spent in the regular classroom.

**Level IV** is designed for a child requiring special education services who spends up to six hours per school day in special education classes in a regular school. The student participates in the general education program when not in the special classes and has access to other services.

**Level V** gives a child all his education in a special education setting within a special wing of a regular school or in a special school for up to six hours per day. The maximum class size for this level is six handicapped students with special education needs per full-time certified special education teacher or an average of nine if a full-time aide is provided.

**Level VI** is placement in a residential setting for the child who requires twenty-four hour special education programming and personal care. Under the regulations of Public Law 94–142, a severely emotionally disturbed child who meets the requirements of the legal definition, who requires twenty-four hour care, and who falls within the age group for which free public education is provided by the state should be eligible for residential placement in an appropriate setting at state expense.

If you can, visit the school the team is recommending for your child. Try to spend the whole day and include interviews with administrators, teachers, and students, as well as observing at least three classes. You should look for evidence that the school utilizes the principles of teaching persons with mental illness outlined below.

# Learning Problems

Children with serious mental illness experience several kinds of general learning problems. The various problems may be experienced to different degrees and in different combinations by specific individuals. The following is a listing of some of the more general types of problems interfering with learning together with brief summaries of some educational responses to these frequently occurring problems.

## Distractibility and Irritability

For some children in the acute phase of a serious mental illness, the world is a confusing place filled with distractions, excessive stimuli, and lack of order. Many children complain of loud noises, extremely bright lights, and distractions caused by the activities of others.

**The Educational Response:** The classroom for these children must emphasize reasonable order and predictability. It must be well organized and nonstressful. This does not mean, however, that the classroom must be boring, totally routine, or inflexible. The structure of the activities in the classroom should be predictable but not rigid.

## The Need for Structure

The child with serious mental illness is also easily frustrated by unnecessary distractions or problems posed in learning. The difficulty of dealing with the symptoms of mental illness leave little energy for dealing with unnecessary obstacles to learning.

**The Educational Response:** The curriculum must be extremely well designed to help the child learn. Objectives must be clearly stated and activities selected so that learning is maximized. The sequence of instruction must be outstanding so that learning proceeds smoothly with as few difficulties as possible. Finally and most importantly, the material must be organized in such a way as to minimize frustration while maximizing interest. The size of the steps in learning must be geared to the ability and interest of the individual learner.

## Damaged Self-Esteem

The self-esteem of the child suffering serious mental illness has often been damaged by the frustrations of the illness, by the degradation of confinement, by frequent denial of normal privileges, by lack of understanding and sympathy, and by the use of psychological and sometimes physical abuse by others. The full extent of such damage has not been adequately assessed by experts but is often significant.

**The Educational Response:** Schooling can be a major method for rebuilding a child's self-esteem. Classes must provide rewards, praise, and encouragement. They must emphasize success and minimize punishment as much as possible. Teachers, classrooms, and curricula must reflect and emphasize confidence in the student's ability to learn. This confidence will generate success and enhance the learner's confidence and self-respect.

## Reduced Motivation

Motivation to learn is a major problem for students suffering a serious mental illness. The student suffers from the depression produced by any serious illness, be it physical or mental. The lack of motivation can also be a direct consequence of the illness. For example, in severe depression, loss of normal feelings of pleasure is a common consequence of the illness. Further, the student with a serious mental illness questions his future and needs reassurance. He may, mistakenly, believe that since he has a mental illness he will never get better and has no reason to learn.

**The Educational Response:** The correct response to the motivation problem is the creation of a classroom atmosphere and curriculum which makes learning as enjoyable and stimulating as possible. Creative writing assignments clearly explained and structured, newspapers and magazines produced and edited by the students, and well organized plays and skits are only a few of the ways that classes can be made stimulating and motivating. Classrooms can be organized to produce creativity and still be predictable and orderly. Another general method of motivating the student which is particularly useful with persons experiencing mental illness is exploration of the individual student's special interests. If the student is interested in music, sports, or art, teachers should be aware of this interest and should relate learning experiences to it. In addition, the special areas of interest can be used as rewards for successful study. Taking the students on hikes, sporting events such as skiing, and providing music lessons can be rewards for excellence. Special trips and excursions can both explore these special interests and can be used as learning activities. For students with mental illness, these activities provide goals that give them the encouragement to succeed in meeting educational problems and the difficulties of coping with their illness in general. While it is true that creativity and motivation are inhibited by serious mental illness, especially during the times when symptoms are active, it is equally true that these qualities are not extinguished. Some creative work of a very high order is produced by persons who are suffering mental illness and all these persons are capable of creative and stimulating responses. Further, they need all the positive experiences they can get.

## Limited Attention Span

Another problem faced by the learner with a mental illness is shortening of the attention span. This problem is quite common.

**The Educational Response:** Educators need to make sure that objectives are clearly stated and reasonable for the time available for instruction. The sequence of instruction must be clear, and frequent evaluation is needed to encourage the student that he is really learning. If the student has a clear idea of what is expected of him and is able to see progress occurring even if the steps are small and the progress is slow, he will continue to work regardless of the difficulty.

### Inadequate Social Relations

Poor relations with peers, with teachers, with visitors, and especially with administrators are common for students with mental illnesses.

**The Educational Response:** In the area of social relations, education can be very beneficial in rewarding efforts to behave appropriately in groups and with other persons. Punishments such as withholding trips, opportunities for participation in some games, or tokens needed to purchase products can be used to improve social behavior if the withholding of these rewards is done to a very limited extent and for very brief periods of time. The use of negative reinforcers such as time-out periods when students may not participate with the class or the use of quiet time when students are placed in areas away from the group may also be used. However, there is a strong tendency to overuse quiet time and time-out periods and to use them to break students' spirits or destroy morale so that the children can be easily manipulated and their behavior overly controlled. Such powerful techniques must be used very sparingly and must be paired with powerful rewards for correct behavior if students are to learn good social skills and to maintain their self-esteem and morale.

No matter what school your child is in, you will want to be certain that they handle the above problems in the ways described. But there is more that you have to take into consideration than just how a school responds to learning problems. You need to consider the school's overall educational approach. Your child is an individual and what is right for another student may not be right for her. Read the following section, decide if that approach is the one followed by the school recommended by your assessment team, and then discuss your findings with them. If you disagree with their choice, tell them why and explain why you would prefer a different educational approach.

# General Educational Approaches

There are four different approaches to education for the mentally ill. These are the *behavioral*, the *psychoeducational*, the *ecological*, and the *eclectic/practical*. The first three of these approaches have identifiable principles and concepts which set them apart from the others.

The fourth approach, the eclectic, is as its name suggests, an approach which incorporates some features of the first three.

## The Behavioral Approach

The behavioral approach is the most frequently used of the approaches with a specific theoretical orientation. It uses the concepts of behavioristic psychology and education often used in programs for both normal students and special education students. The approach gets its name from the idea that education should be a shaping of the behavior of the individual in specific, predetermined ways. Behaviorism uses rewards and punishments to encourage persons to perform certain desired actions and to avoid undesired ones. Psychologists reasoned that humans only learned to do things for which they were rewarded or which were followed by some kind of pleasurable experience

In general, behaviorism requires beginning a learning sequence with children by using concrete reinforcers such as candy and play periods. Later it is possible to substitute stars or tokens which could be claimed for so much candy or free time. Still later, the stars and tokens may be phased out and the children would do school work simply for praise, grades, and knowledge of correct results. From time to time it might be necessary to add some concrete rewards again when work was unusually difficult or boring.

Today virtually all teachers are well trained in the theory and use of rewards or reinforcers and incorporate these methods regularly in their teaching. The judicious use of rewards has been found to be one of the most powerful teaching devices to shape the behavior of normal and special children and adults.

As these techniques and their power have become better known, they have been used much more frequently. If your child has made a grade of "A" on a subject in which he previously had received a "B," it is very wise to reinforce that behavior strongly by praising him in clear terms and giving him that baseball mitt or trip that he wanted. If you want to make a good impression on someone, nod and smile vigorously when they are talking about their interests. The power of reinforcers to shape behavior is perhaps the best established fact of educational psychology today.

Applications of the behavioral approach range from the simple use of rewards to increase some aspect of learning to total programs that control all aspects of education through the use of a behavioral system. In the case of some residential schools for the severely mentally ill, the entire life as well as education of the child is controlled by behavioral systems. This usually involves setting up a so-called "token economy."

Practically all the child's property is taken away to make him dependent on the token economy. If the child wants a bar of soap or a clean towel or a new tube of toothpaste, the products must be earned by gaining points which can be exchanged for tokens which in turn can be exchanged for the items desired. Points are earned for free time, for trips, for new lamps, etc. By controlling the entire life of the child, the school has more power to shape his behavior. The right to attend classes is often preferred to the boredom of being by oneself on the residential wards. Class attendance becomes dependent on the child performing the type of behavior desired by the staff.

Clearly, the more extreme forms of the use of the behavioral approach raise moral and ethical questions about the degree of control of behavior that should be permitted under such systems. Because a system such as the one described above establishes total control over all aspects of a person's life, it is an example of the unethical use of the behavioral approach, unless it is used with patients who pose a continual danger to themselves or others. Yet, most of the residential centers for the treatment of the mentally ill and a sizable percentage of the residential schools use these total behavioral systems.

Less extreme forms of behavioral control, which permit the student the basic freedoms and rights to property of the average individual and use rewards primarily to encourage better behavior, are acceptable and effective ways to improve performance. Schools which begin with the premise that an individual waives his rights to personal property and fundamental freedoms when he enters an institution are improper except in a totalitarian society and should not be permitted to operate in such a manner. An obvious exception to this rule would be an alternative school for students who have extreme discipline problems which bring them into conflict with the law.

## Characteristics of the Behavioral Approach:
1. Heavy reliance on the use of reinforcement techniques.

2. Specific objectives (behavioral objectives) describing in great detail the specific kinds of behavior to be taught pupils at each step in a detailed program.
3. Emphasis on practice and demonstration of the skills to be taught. Learning is not considered to have occurred until the learner can demonstrate the skill.
4. Frequent evaluations and detailed records of achievement, including maintenance of profiles detailing the child's progress or lack of progress.

## Advantages of the Behavioral Approach:

1. The behavioral approach is a powerful technique and properly applied can increase learning, performance, and motivation.
2. The behavioral approach is well organized so that it tends to respond to the need for structure demonstrated by most students with mental illness.
3. The behavioral approach has clear goals so that instruction is well focused.
4. Evaluation tends to be detailed and precise because the goals and objectives are clearly specified.

## Disadvantages of the Behavioral Approach:

1. Excessive dependence on the behavioral approach in an inappropriate setting can lead to practices which infringe on the basic freedoms of the individual.
2. There is a tendency to over-emphasize basic skills and underemphasize creative response because the creative responses cannot be programmed or predicted as well as is desired under a behavioral approach.
3. There is a tendency for the system to become too mechanical and automatic so that little imagination or thought is used in the application of the system.

## Evaluation of the Behavioral Approach:

The behavioral approach has many strengths and relatively few weaknesses. If the program you are considering applies it with imagination, in moderation, and with humanity, it can be a powerful and effective method of educating your child.

## The Ecological Approach

The ecological approach is enjoying considerable prominence in the 1980s. It emphasizes the role of environmental stress in mental illness and assumes that mental illness is a result of that environmental stress. The child's environment is surveyed to locate problem areas. Once the locale and the nature of the problem are identified, the educational team determines an appropriate intervention. If an unreasonable degree of stress occurs in school because of a particular problem, the educator attempts to solve the problem and reduce the stress. If a problem occurs in the home, the problem is identified and a solution is attempted. For example, the child with mental illness may have no outside activities in the home setting. A solution might be found in getting the child involved in a swimming club or some other structured activity.

### Evaluation of the Ecological Approach:

The assumption that a child's whole environment must be taken into consideration is absolutely correct. The home life and the role of the family must be included in educational and treatment plans. While it is not true that the family *causes* mental illness, it is true that the family must work with the child suffering mental illness and must do all that can be done for the child. Further, the family needs assistance in dealing with the problems of coping with the child. The ecological perspective, properly used, puts emphasis on meeting the needs of the family and providing specific ways to support the role of the family. The approach emphasizes the interaction of the child, the school, the health care providers, and the family.

The ecological approach is not a sufficiently distinctive approach to be used exclusively. Rather this approach should be incorporated as an aspect of all planning and work with the mentally ill.

## The Psychoeducational Approach

The third approach to education of the mentally ill has been called the psychoeducational approach. There are two basic assumptions to this approach. The first is that mental illness is a consequence of inadequate or improper development. The second is that education and psychotherapy can work together as allies in helping the mentally ill individual.

This approach calls for educational and therapeutic strategies that are developed by physicians, educators, and social workers acting as a team. The role of psychoeducational programs is to bring together the therapeutic efforts of the health team with the educational efforts of the school. Through the psychoeducational approach, a child's development is reconstructed by an excellent personal rapport between the teacher and the student, by dealing with the feelings and attitudes of the student, by attention to special interests of the student, and by the development of improved social relationships between the student and others.

The teacher and the school work with the health care team by using the school as a laboratory where the student can work through feelings of inadequacy, mistrust, dependency, shame, and inferiority to restore pride and self-confidence. This approach involves the school in the following activities:

1. Attention to feelings and emotions as well as the rational faculties;
2. Emphasis on developing good interpersonal relations and social skills;
3. Emphasis on developing creative skills as well as such skills as understanding, comprehension, and application;
4. Emphasis on skills needed to work effectively in the larger community outside the school; and
5. Emphasis on art, music, drama, and play as needed vehicles for reworking the personality.

The psychoeducational approach requires relatively low student/teacher ratios so that the teacher can get to know each student well and can design programs which address the problems of each individual student. Ideally, the ratio should be about one teacher and one teacher's aide to nine students in each class of emotionally disturbed students (Level V). Without a teacher's aide, the ratio should be one teacher for each six students.

According to the highest standards of the psychoeducational approach, classes should not only ensure that basic skills such as writing, computing, and reading are mastered, but should also stress creative work, group work, moral development, and critical thinking. The goal of the school is not merely the development of logical processes but rather the development of a fully functioning, well integrated, and, therefore, sane human being.

### Strengths of the Psychoeducational Approach:

Because of its broad scope, the psychoeducational approach demands more of education than does either the behavioristic or the ecological model. It aims for the reconstruction of a damaged or inadequately developed personality. It also incorporates much of the concern with the total environment of the individual which is the thrust of the ecological model.

### Weaknesses of the Psychoeducational Approach:

The problem with this approach is that it, like the ecological model, assumes an incorrect cause for serious mental illness. Both the ecological and the psychoeducational approaches assume that the family plays a major role in causing mental illness. Serious mental illness has a biological basis. While a mental illness can be triggered by stress or the environment, it cannot be caused by it.

### Evaluation of the Psychoeducational Approach:

This approach has value because it recommends a form of education that addresses the total development of the child—that is, an education that assumes that concern with attitudes, feelings, and values is as important as concern with cognitive development. The psychoeducational concepts should be incorporated into all educational efforts for persons suffering from mental illness.

## The Eclectic/Practical Approach

The fourth approach is not really a unique approach at all. The eclectic/practical approach simply combines elements of the other approaches. It assumes that serious mental illness has a biological basis but must be treated through a combination of medical, psychological, social, and educational procedures. Serious mental illness has wide-ranging impact on the person affected. Consequently, a broad variety of interventions are needed. The teacher must work closely with the child's health team. This team has as their shared goal, the restoration of the child to normal functioning.

### Characteristics of the Eclectic/Practical Approach:

1. Serious mental illness is assumed to be a result of biological factors which require medical intervention, including treatment with appropriate medications.

2. Although the cause of serious mental illness is assumed to be biological with a possible genetic component, the practical approach recognizes that the illness may be triggered by stress in any aspect of the environment.
3. Although mental illness usually requires treatment through medication (in those cases where effective medication is available), treatment must also include behavioral therapy, social therapy, and education.
4. The educational concepts of this approach are broad and make use of reinforcement (both positive and negative), structured learning environments, attention to feelings and social development, encouragement of creative activities, maintenance of a broad range of interests, and attention to patterns of stress in the environment.

**Evaluation of the Eclectic/Practical Approach:**
The eclectic/practical approach is geared to the specific child. It uses the reinforcement techniques and the determination of specific objectives of the behavioral approach, the emphasis on working with feelings and social development of the psychoeducational approach, and the emphasis on intervention in the total environment of the ecological approach. It can combine the strengths of each of the other three approaches while avoiding their weaknesses.

# The Need For Educational Programs For People Who Have Recovered From Mental Illness

The incidence of serious mental illness is very high. More hospital space is taken up by the severely mentally ill than by patients suffering from cancer, lung, and heart diseases combined. Since the prognosis for serious mental illness is that approximately 75 percent will recover sufficiently to perform responsible work, it is clear that at any given point in time, there are a large number of persons in society who have recovered or are recovering from a mental illness.

Frequently mental illness strikes our young people between the ages of fourteen and twenty-five. The average period of institutionalization is about two years. Probably about half of those persons suffering from mental illness during those years lose a significant amount of education because of institutionalization. In addition to this loss, these young people also frequently lose self-confidence, self-respect, social skills, and the ability to earn a living.

There is a great need in our society to provide education for those who have lost educational opportunities due to mental illness. People who have been institutionalized with mental illness during the middle school, high school, and college years should be given an opportunity to return to school once they have recovered. No one should be penalized educationally because of an illness, whether that illness affects them physically or mentally.

The federal government should make available funds to the states to provide education through the first two years of college or equivalent vocational training for persons who have been institutionalized during the years when they would have been attending school. This type of remedial special education is desperately needed.

## Conclusion

This chapter has covered some of the things you will have to consider when looking into educational alternatives for your child and has shown you four educational approaches that are frequently used. It will be up to you to try to find the best educational approach available for your child. Work with her assessment team; make your wishes known and your reasons. What you do can be very important in seeing that your child gets the education she needs so she can be ready to go forward in her life when she recovers from her illness.

### REFERENCES

Apter, Steven J. and Jane Close Conoley. *Childhood Behavior Disorders and Emotional Disturbances*. Englewood Cliffs, NJ: Prentice-Hall, 1984.

Apter, Steven J. *Troubled Children: Troubled Systems*. New York: Pergamon Press, 1982.

Egeland, J. A., D.S. Gerhard, D. L. Pauls, J. N. Sussex, K.K. Kid, R. A. Cleona, A. M. Hestter, and Houseman. "Bipolar Affective Disorders Linked to DNA markers on Chromosome 11." *Nature* 325, no. 26 (February, 1987): 783–87.

Fass, Larry A. *The Emotionally Disturbed Child*. Springfield, IL: Chas. C. Thomas, 1975.

McDowell, Richard L., Gary W. Adamson, and Frank H. Wood. *Teaching Emotionally Disturbed Children*. Boston: Little, Brown and Company, 1982.

Mosier, Doris Burkett & Ruth Burkett Park. *Teacher-Therapist: A Text-Handbook for Teachers of Emotionally Impaired Children*. Santa Monica, CA: Goodyear Publishing Co., Inc. 1971.

Reinert, Henry R. *Children in Conflict*. 2d ed. St. Louis: The C.V. Mosby Company, 1980.

Towns, Peyton. *Educating Disturbed Adolescents: Theory and Practice*. New York: Grune & Stratton, 1981

# Parent Statements

Kim is in a special residential school now and doing very well. We are slowly building a new parent/child relationship, but we remain very angry at those early days when we wasted so much time focusing on a "family" problem when it was really a biological problem with Kim. All those years we could have been trying to get help for our daughter and instead we listened to the wrong "experts." If I have any advice for parents reading this, it is to trust your instincts about your child and find professionals who will help you do what you think is right for her.

=❀=

Johnny was seven years old when his grandmother brought him to the outpatient therapy department of a university hospital. Johnny was afraid to go to school. A psychiatric nurse visited the school, the treatment team tested him and it turned out that Johnny had learning problems and needed a special school. The team worked with the officials and got him into a different school. It took a while but he's doing a lot better.

=❀=

It's so sad. Barry is so smart; almost a genius. He could speak five languages when he was eleven. He wanted to go in the diplomatic corps. Then he got sick. He still wants an education but the pressure of the assignments is too much for him. He has another manic spell. He's twenty-two now. He wants to go to college. I wish there was some way for him to get the education he missed all through those teen years when he was so sick.

=❀=

Terry only had to be in some special classes. She could handle junior high some of the time but she needed a quieter classroom with less stress. It didn't seem so much to ask, particularly with her depression, but I had to get a lawyer to get her the proper placement.

The school did everything. They told me Mike was hyperactive; they told me what kind of program he should be in, and then they went ahead and planned the whole thing. He's a pretty good student now. I couldn't be happier.

He gets so discouraged doing janitorial jobs. That's all he's trained for now. He's still smart. Why can't our country find some way to educate him so he can get a job that better matches his values and intellect?

Patti had enough trouble going back to high school after being in a mental hospital for a couple of months. In a small town, everybody gets to know a thing like that. The other kids treated her like she was from Mars. On top of trying to learn how to study again, she had to face all that teasing. There should be something in her special education program that teaches her how to get along with people better.

Before Alice was hospitalized she was one of the most popular girls in school—for fifteen minutes per group. She ran through two-day friends like mad. She just didn't have any idea how to make a friend and develop a relationship. I think learning how to get along with people is the most important thing she can learn. I look at social skills a lot when I evaluate an educational program for her.

Her father just assumed she was stupid. The school was all the time sending home complaints about her work. Finally she got a teacher who realized she had problems and requested an evaluation.

The right school can make all the difference in how your child views learning.

Our county wouldn't do anything for George. We were all alone. We knew something was wrong; we got him on medication, we got him a therapist, and we got our act together at home but school was still a problem. A big problem! Finally we just yanked him out and put him in a private school that was willing to work with us. Naturally, once we did that, we had to pay for everything ourselves. We just didn't know any better. Now I tell everybody to find out what your rights are and then fight to get them.

## SEVEN
=❀=

# Handling a Suicide Crisis

### TERRY ROSENBERG

If your child has attempted suicide or has threatened it, then you must act now to prevent a tragedy of unbearable proportions. There is no pain more overwhelming than that of losing a child and when that child takes his own life, the pain is even worse. Any threat or attempt at suicide must be taken very seriously if you are not to lose your child. There are signs for you to look for and things for you to do. If your child gets the help he needs in time, then the chances are excellent that he will come through this life-threatening time to a full, rewarding future.

Your child has signalled his need for help either by attempting suicide or threatening it. Now you need to find out what to do to make sure he doesn't carry through with killing himself.

First, you need to know that you are not alone in your concern for your child. Thousands of parents join you in this nightmare of uncertainty and anguish. More than five thousand teenagers committed suicide in 1985 and in the last twenty years, teen suicides have increased 400 percent. It is the second leading cause of death in adolescents, ranking just behind accidents. And many of these officially designated accidents are strongly suspected of being suicides. Experts agree that the rate of suicide is much higher than the statistics lead us to believe, and those are horrifying enough.

It is very possible that your child's desire to die is only one symptom of his mental illness. Chemically caused depression, psychosis, or personality disorders can trigger suicide attempts. These attempts can also be triggered by the hormonal changes and pressures most teenagers go through.

The teenage years are an agony of emotions run rampant. Ask yourself if you would ever want to be seventeen again. Many of us wouldn't! We remember the pain, the embarrassment, the fear at having to grow up, the worry that we would never measure up to our parents' expectations. The internal pressures on adolescents are probably the greatest they will ever have to live through. These emotions can be based in reality, or in their vision of reality. We may be overwhelmingly proud of our children, and think they are wonderful, and yet they may think we see them as failures. It is all part of the mixture of hormones and emotions that they are trying to deal with.

Our youngsters have all the emotions we had at their age, plus the stresses of modern society. And those stresses can be awesome in themselves. The family structure has changed drastically. Schools and neighborhoods are overrun with drugs and alcohol. We are a nation in search of an identity, and our teenagers are struggling both with their own identities and the lack of structure in the institutions around them.

The pressures on our kids are things we must take into account before we say, "These are the best years of your life. No responsibilities—you'll never have it so good again." To your teenager, those words could really be the "kiss of death." These are not good years for him, and he can't express how unhappy he is. You must understand how hard it is for him and find ways to help him live through this and build for his future.

> *The Duncans found that out for themselves the hard way. One night they were awakened by a crash and the sound of breaking glass in their bathroom. Mae ran in and found her seventeen-year-old son, Johnny, sprawled on the floor, fragments of the broken bathroom glass sprinkled around him, the shower rod bent, and a belt knotted around his throat.*
>
> *He had tried to kill himself. Her beautiful, adored child had tried to destroy himself. Her mind couldn't comprehend it. She pushed the knowledge away even as the rescue squad bandaged Johnny's cuts and looked at the bruises on his neck.*
>
> *In the emergency room no one mentioned suicide, no police came, and she and her husband, Richard, began the dangerous*

*playacting that it really hadn't happened. Johnny was literally dying to talk about it, but his parents were refusing to face the reality.*

*"I'm sorry, Mommy. I didn't mean to hurt you. I won't do it again." Johnny sobbed all the way back home and Mae wanted desperately to believe him. So much so that she tried to soothe her son. "It's all right, darling. I know you won't. It'll be all right."*

But it wasn't all right. Johnny needed help. He had tried to kill himself once and he might try again if he didn't get the help he needed. About half the people who attempt suicide try again if they don't get help. You can help your child be in the 50 percent of those who go on with their lives. You must know what to look for.

There are certain warning signs that you should take into account when evaluating your child's level of vulnerability. These are the factors that would make a professional label your child a high suicide risk.

## Warning Signs

1. Loss of friends or status;
2. Lack of outside interests;
3. Violent behavior;
4. Behavior and character disorders;
5. Alcohol and/or drug abuse;
6. Family stress;
7. Homosexuality;
8. Fear of punishment;
9. Running away;
10. A family history of suicide;
11. Trouble concentrating;
12. Poor school performance;
13. Immediate access to the means to kill himself;
14. Loneliness, poor self-esteem, isolation;
15. Psychiatric disorder;
16. Loss of a loved one through death;
17. Slovenly appearance;
18. Pregnancy;
19. Complaints of aches and pains;
20. Chronic boredom;

21. Illness or disability;
22. Other teenage suicides—there is a chain reaction where suicides come in clusters;
23. Suddenly putting his affairs in order—giving away valued possessions, or paying off debts.

## Depression

A major factor that increases the chances of your adolescent attempting suicide is depression. Current research indicates that most depression is genetically linked. In other words, the tendency toward depression is inherited. While your child may have gone through most of his childhood in a relatively serene fashion, it is possible that some environmental factor can trigger an episode of depression. If this occurs, then your child is at risk to attempt suicide. There are diagnostic tests and experts available to help your child, and it is essential that you have your child evaluated as soon as possible. An effective treatment plan must be developed and monitored by a competent professional. Medication in combination with other therapy may be necessary.

If you are not sure if your child is depressed, ask yourself the following questions:

1. Does he eat more or less than usual?
2. Does he have disturbed sleep patterns or sleep an excessive amount?
3. Does he say that life is not worth living, or that he is worthless?
4. Has he lost weight?
5. Does he hide out away from his friends and family?
6. Is he alone a lot of the time?
7. Has his work in school gotten worse?
8. Has his behavior gotten worse?
9. Does he refuse to talk with you any more, saying he's fine and to leave him alone?

If you can answer "yes" to some of these questions, then you have a depressed child and it is important that you take his problem seriously. When you add his suicide attempt or threat to depression, you have a potential disaster on your hands.

# Family Stress

Another area that might add to your child's wish to die is family stress. Studies have shown it to be the most important *environmental* factor associated with suicidal behavior in children and adolescents. This does not mean you caused your child's problems, but you may be a factor. If so you may be able to do something about it. A family crisis is often the precipitating cause of suicide.

In homes with a history of violence, childhood suicide rates increase dramatically. If your child has been physically or sexually abused, he is in the high risk group.

If a member of your family has committed suicide, your child is more prone to try to kill himself. It may be more acceptable to him, or he may wish to be "like" the deceased member of your family.

*It took Richard's newly widowed mother to bring the reality of Johnny's suicide attempt home to the Duncans. It was impossible to keep the truth from her since she made her usual visit the next day and saw her grandson's cuts and bruises. Her shock and her demand that something be done awakened Johnny's parents to the dangers before them.*

*They were suddenly desperate to do something, anything to make sure that their son would be all right. They called their family doctor, who urged them to get psychiatric help for Johnny at once. They set up an appointment with a specialist in adolescent disorders, but Richard was not going to be there. It was time for his monthly sales trip and he would be gone for two weeks. The Duncans were faced with their first decision.*

*Would they pretend that everything would wait until Richard got back from his trip, or would they realize the urgency of the situation and change his schedule so he could be with the rest of the family for that crucial first evaluation?*

# What To Do

You cannot afford to delude yourself that everything will be all right. It might not be if you don't act now. The very first thing you do is get rid of anything that you think *might* pose a physical danger to your child. **GET RID OF YOUR GUNS!** Over 60 percent of all known suicides are the result of guns. Don't throw the gun away, take it to the nearest police station, where they can dispose of it safely.

While you can't completely safeguard your home, you can keep all aspirin, Tylenol, and prescription drugs out of reach of your child. If he has a headache, you go get the aspirin and give him the recommended dose and then take the bottle and put it where he can't find it. Check the bottle periodically to make sure that significant numbers of pills haven't disappeared.

Take your sharp knives and put them away safely. Make sure that there are no hoses around that could fit over the exhaust pipe of your car. Be alert and keep a close eye on your youngster. Don't leave him alone for long periods of time.

Next, find some professional help. Work with your local mental health agency or a private therapist to help your child talk about his problems and reassure him that you will do everything you can to make the situation better for him. And mean it. If you have to change your work schedule, like Richard, do it. If you have to listen to problems that you think trivial, then listen anyway. They are not trivial problems to your child and he needs to explain what they are and get your acceptance that they are important to him.

Take the time to evaluate what is really important to you. Does your child have to have the good grades you didn't get in order to become that professional you wanted to be? Does he know how much you love him and how your life will be destroyed if he destroys his? Tell him; he needs to know. Tell him again. Reassure him that you are not ashamed of him, or angry that he is suicidal, but you are determined that he live and feel better. Promise him that you will do everything you can to help this bad time pass for him and help him to a happier future. Remind him over and over that there is an end to any tunnel and he can be happier and will be happier. You will help him. But this happier life can only happen if he lives.

You will have to coordinate the care your child gets. You will have to case manage things with his school, his therapist, his physician, and his family. Generally speaking, there are seven categories of suicide types. You will find this information helpful when working as a case manager. You may be able to fit your child into one of these categories and then be better able to plan what to do to help him. The categories are:

1. Psychosis or personality disintegration–he displays psychotic

symptoms (hallucinations, delusions, etc.).

2. Self-homicide—your child is filled with unacceptable rage toward someone else, which he turns in on himself.
3. Retaliation for real or imagined abandonment—he feels threatened by rejection and acts first to compensate for his feelings of helplessness and to "beat you to the punch."
4. Blackmail and/or manipulation—he uses suicidal threats or gestures as power plays.
5. He thinks of death as a way to rejoin a dead loved one.
6. He feels so guilty for his actions that he tries to die to atone for his sins.
7. A cry for help—he can think of no other way to express his pain or to call for help.

*Johnny's therapist spent the first hour listening to Johnny say that his parents were great and he had no complaints. She never challenged that, she just nodded and then asked a few questions of Johnny's parents. When did Johnny's grandfather die? Had anyone in the family committed suicide? Once she had an idea of the family history, she started to find out how the family worked as a unit. She learned that Richard was away a lot and that Mae was very involved with their younger son. Johnny was on his own a great deal. He seemed to feel special pressure to always be the "good" boy. Everyone envied the Duncans for this hard working, serious teenager who always seemed calm and in control.*

*The Duncan men had a history of internalizing their emotions and of borderline depressive behavior. The Duncans would have to have some assessments made and would need to explore the possibility of treatment for a depressive disorder which might include the use of antidepressant medications. Johnny was raised to think that expressing negative emotions was wrong and unmanly.*

*The therapist explained this to the Duncans and, predictably, Richard reacted strongly, denying that this was his pattern. When Mae hesitantly agreed that Richard did behave like that, her husband acted as if he had been betrayed. Johnny just got quieter and quieter, torn between trying to protect his mother and not confronting his father. There were serious issues that the Duncans were going to have to work out.*

*The therapist emphasized to the Duncans that while it was obvious that they all loved each other deeply, there were issues to face and that all three of them would need to work on them in her office. Outside her office they were to try to communicate in supportive ways, helping each other and recognizing the problems, but were to avoid all blame and confrontation. They were to make the home as safe and loving as possible for John, and he was to work with her on ways to express himself. The Duncans left her office thinking that what she asked was easy enough, but it proved harder than they had thought.*

# Communication

*The Duncans made a family pact not to pretend that the suicide attempt had never happened but to face it and use it to work on problems within the family. The family and a tendency toward depression were only two factors in Johnny's unhappiness with himself and his world. He was also getting ready to graduate from high school and was trying to cope with having had his long-term girlfriend break up with him. It was a lonely time for him at school and the world of college loomed as a potential danger zone for him. He needed to work on verbalizing his feelings and to start finding new ways to express his emotions.*

One of the keys to defusing the dangers for your child is to get him to talk. He may not be able to talk to you, but he can try to talk to a therapist, a valued family friend, or a mentor. It is up to you to see that these avenues open up for him. Always let him know you want to listen, you want to understand, and that you love him.

While you are working with your child, there is the outside world to fend off. Your family will ask questions and well-meaning friends will look for answers to your distress. It is up to you to decide what you will tell them and how much. Since many Americans feel that suicide is a shameful act, you may try to protect your child as much as possible from society's condemnation. At the same time, there are people with a legitimate right to know. Only you as a family can decide who these people are. Remember, you will need someone to talk to; the pain is too intense for you not to confide in someone. When you do talk to people, you will want to have as much accurate information as possible so that you are all working from the same basic knowledge to help you and your child. Here are some facts you need to know.

## Facts

1. Most people who have killed themselves have talked about suicide or given clues that they were thinking of dying as a way out of their problems.
2. People thinking about suicide are usually not sure that death is the right answer for them and often are looking for help and a better answer.
3. As we have discussed, depression is often a factor when people think about suicide, but not all people who try to kill themselves seem depressed. Many of them seem to be happy; perhaps because they have decided to "end all their problems" and they have nothing more to worry about.
4. There is a definite correlation between alcoholism and suicidal behavior. Alcoholics are very prone to suicide attempts.
5. Not all people who try to commit suicide have a mental illness.
6. Even people who are very serious about suicide and actually try to kill themselves usually feel suicidal for only a short time. If they receive the help they need, they usually go on to live the rest of their lives without another episode involving suicide or an attempted suicide.
7. It is a good idea to try to get your child to talk about his suicidal feelings. That way he can verbalize some of his anxieties and tensions and you may be able to make him feel better about his problems and less liable to use suicide as a way out.
8. There are no class or economic boundaries to suicide. Rich and poor alike try suicide.
9. You must be particularly alert for the first three months after your child has begun to recover from a deep depression. While he was in the depths of his depression he may not have had the energy to actively try suicide but as he is feeling better, he is more likely to try suicide. Beware of sudden bursts

of sunshine for no reason, he may have decided to end it all and be feeling overwhelming relief.

10. Girls more often use guns than drugs to kill themselves.

## Take Care Of Yourself

You must learn to communicate with your child in order to hear what is happening with him and help him. But you will need help, too. You are so frightened you can't breathe and yet you must go on for the sake of the whole family. The pressures overwhelm you. You are angry: at yourself, at your spouse, and at your child for what has happened to you and the fearful reality you are living. All these emotions must be dealt with if you are to be able to deal with your child. Throughout this book the authors have emphasized ways to handle stress; they remain the same no matter what the source of the stress:

1. Take time for yourself;
2. Find people to talk to about your feelings;
3. Exercise;
4. Take each day as it comes;
5. Congratulate yourself for every forward step, no matter how small;
6. Learn from every mistake;
7. Get out and do things.

There are places to go for more information and guidance. Every county must, by law, have a suicide prevention center or mental health agency. You can call information to get the phone number of the one in your area. Suicide prevention centers can give you a wealth of information.

If you feel you want more information, you can contact:

Youth Suicide National Center
1825 Eye Street, NW, Suite 400
Washington, DC 20006
202/429–2016

Suicide in young people is such a big problem that more and more resources are being devoted to solving this problem. Schools have outreach programs, counties have mental health centers, and many religious organizations have special programs to help us deal with suicide.

In 1985 President Reagan designated June as "Youth Suicide Prevention Month." Our government leaders are becoming more aware of the scope of this problem. Congress passed a bill providing funds for grants for youth suicide prevention programs. Another bill directed the National Institute of Mental Health to develop and distribute information on suicide prevention. A national task force has been established to study youth suicide. All this is being done in response to the enormity of the problem. You are facing suicide as a parent, but it is also a national problem. Together, perhaps we can all make a difference and our children will be free to grow to adulthood.

## REFERENCES

Beebe, John III. "Treatment of the Suicidal Patient." In *Psychiatric Treatment: Crisis, Clinic and Consultation*, edited by C.P. Rosenbaum and J.E. Beebe, III, 42–62, 19–41. New York: McGraw-Hill Book Company, 1975.

Berlin, Irving. "Prevention of Adolescent Suicide Among Some Native American Tribes." *Adolescent Psychiatry* 12 (1985).

Browning, Charles. "Epidemiology of Suicide: Firearms." *Comprehensive Psychiatry* 15, no. 6 (November/December 1974).

Carlson, Gabrielle and Dennis Cantwell. "Suicidal Behavior and Depression in Children and Adolescents." *American Academy of Child Psychology* 21, no. 4 (1982).

Clayton, Paula. "Suicide." *Psychiatric Clinics of North America* 8, no. 2 (June 1985).

Copland, Arthur. "Teenage Suicide–The Five- Year Metro Dade County Experience from 1979 Until 1983." *Forensic Science International* 28 (1985).

Davis, John. "Suicidal Crises in Schools." *School Psychology Review* 14, no. 3 (1985).

Egeland, Janice and James Sussex. "Suicide and Family Loading for Affective Disorders." *The Journal of the American Medical Association* 254, no. 7 (August 16, 1985).

Frederick, Calvin. "Current Trends in Suicidal Behavior in the United States." *American Journal of Psychotherapy* 32 (1978).

Frederick, Calvin. "Trends in Mental Health." *Keynote Magazine* 4, no. 3 (May 1976).

Galambos, Nancy and Roger Dixon. "Adolescent Abuse and the Development of Personal Sense of Control." *Child Abuse and Neglect* 8 (1984).

Galanter, Marc and Ricardo Castaneda. "Self- Destructive Behavior in the Substance Abuser." *Psychiatric Clinics of North America* 8, no. 2 (June 1985).

Hendin, Herbert. "Suicide: A Review of New Directions in Research." *Hospitals and Community Psychiatry* 37, no. 2 (February 1986).

Holinger, Paul. "Adolescent Suicide: An Epidemiological Study of Recent Trends." *American Psychiatric Association* 135, no. 6 (1978).

Hopper, Kim and Sally Guttmacher. "Rethinking Suicide: Notes Toward a Critical Epidemiology." *International Journal of Health Services* 9, no. 3 (1979).

Kosky, Robert. "Childhood Suicidal Behavior." *Journal of Child Psychiatry* 24, no. 3 (1983).

Markush, Robert and Alfred Bartolucci. "Firearms and Suicide in the United States." *American Journal of Public Health* 74 (1984).

Pallikhathayil, Leonie and Angela McBride-Barrow. "Suicide Attempts." *Journal of Psychosocial Nursing* 24, no. 18 (August 1986).

Peck, Michael. "Adolescent Suicide." *Audio Digest* 12, no. 18 (1983).

Pfeffer, Cynthia. "The Family System of Suicidal Children."*American Journal of Psychotherapy* 35, no. 3 (July 1981).

Pferrer, Cynthia. "Self-Destructive Behavior in Children and Adolescents." *Psychiatric Clinics of North America* 8, no. 2 (June 1985).

Pferrer, Cynthia et al. "Suicidal Behavior in Latency- Age Children." *American Academy of Child Psychiatry* 18 (1979).

Quick, Mary Ellen. "New Training Videodisc on Suicide." *Alcohol, Drug Abuse, and Mental Health* 12, no. 5 (May 1986).

Rosenbaum, Milton and Joseph Richman. "Suicide: The Role of Hostility and Death Wishes from the Family and Significant Others." *American Journal of Psychiatry* 126, no. 11 (May 1970).

Ross, Charlotte and Russel A. Lee. "Suicide in Youth and What You Can Do About It: A Guide for School Personnel." Printed by Courtesy of the Kiwanis Club of San Mateo, California.Sabbath, Joseph. "The Suicidal Adolescent– The Expendable Child." *Journal of the American Academy of Child Psychiatry* 8 (1982).

Sandler-Cohen, Roni et al. "Life Stress and Symptomotology: Determinants of Suicidal Behavior." *Journal of the American Academy of Child Psychiatry* 21, no. 2 (1982).

Shaffer, David and Prudence Fisher. "The Epidemiology of Suicide in Children and Young Adolescents." *American Academy of Child Psychiatry* 20 (1981).

Silver, Barbara et al. "The 1990 Objectives for the Nation for Control of Stress and Violent Behavior: Progress Report." *Public Health Reports* 99, no. 4 (July–August 1984).

Simkin, Deborah. "Teenage Suicide–What Do We Have To Offer?" *Journal of The Louisiana State Medical Society* 138, no. 2 (February 1986).

Smith, Kim and Sylvia Crawford. "Suicidal Behavior Among 'Normal' High School Students." Paper presented at the Fourth Annual Conference on Suicide of Adults and Youth, September 14, 1984.

Sudak, Howard et al. "Adolescent Suicide: An Overview." *American Journal of Psychotherapy* 38, no. 3 (July 1984).

Toolan, James. "Suicide in Children and Adolescents." *American Journal of Psychotherapy* 29 (1975).

Wilson, Patricia. "Teenage Suicide–A Review of the Literature, seminar paper for the University of Maryland, School of Nursing."*Morbidity and Mortality Weekly Report* 134, no. 24 (June 21, 1985).

Centers for Disease Control. "Perspectives in Disease Prevention and Health Promotion." *Morbidity and Mortality Weekly Report* 32, no. 35 (September 9, 1983).

Centers for Disease Control. "Perspectives in Disease Prevention and Health Promotion." *Morbidity and Mortality Weekly Report* 254, no. 4 (July 26, 1985).

Centers for Disease Control. "Youth Suicide Surveillance." Washington, D.C.: U.S. Dept. of Health and Human Services–Publication Service, Summary 1970–1980, November 1986.

Centers for Disease Control. "The Task Force on Youth Suicide: Implementation Plans: Preliminary Recommendations." Washington, D.C.: U.S. Dept. of Health and Human Services, November 18, 1986.

99th Congress, 2nd Session. Bills, H.R. 4650, S.J. Res. 266, H.R. 1243.

The American Association of Suicidology. *Before It's Too Late: What To Do When Someone You Know Attempts Suicide.*

Suicide Prevention and Crisis Center of San Mateo County, California/The American Association of Suicidology. *Suicide in Youth and What You Can Do About It: A Guide for Students.* West Point, PA: Merck Sharp & Dohme.

U.S. Department of Health and Human Services. *National Conference on Strategies for Prevention of Youth Suicide;* Implementation Plans from Conference Workshop.

# Parent Statements

Ed lay around all winter and didn't do much of anything. I figured it was just teenage stuff and didn't worry too much about it. Then one day he tried to kill himself. We couldn't believe it. How could we have been so blind about him? He was really sick but we didn't know anything about depression.

Becky was so upset when her boyfriend killed himself that I got worried about her. I called the suicide prevention line and found out what to do. I talked with her, got her to counseling, enlisted every relative I could find. She's better now and even told me once that I had saved her life.

Its terrifying how thin that line is between doing the right thing for your child and having him dead. If I had walked in five minutes later, he would have been dead.

My son, Jim, was in the state hospital and diagnosed as having depression. We had some initial trouble with the staff but we finally ended up on an upbeat note. He got stabilized on medication, learned a lot about himself, and was able to start planning a life for himself. Not everything turns out bad!

=❀=

My mother-in-law is convinced that it's all my fault that our son shot himself. He used my gun to do it. It's terrible enough to try and live with the suicide of your oldest child, much less have to listen to people tell you it's all your fault.

=❀=

Jennie was in the hospital and the psychiatrist there said that she'd be all right if she learned how to talk with us. All we had to do was open the lines of communication. We brought her home and went into therapy with her. Then she tried to kill herself again. This time I insisted that she get a full evaluation and we found out she had severe clinical depression. She went on Lithium and suddenly she is a functioning teenager again. We all still go to therapy to work on a better relationship, but now she's well enough to work with us.

≡✻≡

After he tried to kill himself, I couldn't sleep. I would get up three and four times every night to go in his room and see if he was still breathing. He was so sweet about it. He'd wake up and reassure me that he was fine. Then I'd go back to my room and cry.

≡✻≡

I just could never understand why he tried to commit suicide. I love him so much. He's my whole life. I tried to explain how important he was to me and he couldn't believe it. He lay in that hospital bed with all those tubes sticking out of him saying over and over that he never realized I cared so much. Now I have to do something to make sure he always remembers how much he's loved and never tries anything like this again.

≡✻≡

EIGHT

# Planning for a Long-Term Illness

CAROL HOWE

This chapter describes ways you can get help and find the community services you need when you learn that your child's mental illness may require long-term care. You will need to understand what your child's diagnosis is, how to select professional care, how to get entitlements, and how to tailor your family's goals for this new element in your lives. Flexibility and knowledge are your keys to a successful long-term plan.

## Why Getting A Diagnosis Is Important

Parents of children or adolescents with "severe emotional disturbance" are seldom given a name for the "emotional disturbance" until late in the course of the illness. This reluctance on the part of the professionals you are paying to give you a diagnosis is perplexing since these same professionals will eagerly assist parents in a diagnosis of diabetes or deafness for their "physically" handicapped child.

Clearly, this refusal on the part of professionals is particularly hard for us to take since it conveys to us that our child has a mental condition so horrible and stigmatizing that it cannot be discussed. It makes us feel even more isolated and can increase our feelings of guilt. Most important, it can delay us in developing a plan effectively to handle our child's illness.

Professionals give several reasons for their failure to inform parents about the nature of their child's mental illness:

1. They are preserving a confidential relationship with the youngster.
2. They believe in a treatment approach that views the parents as patients who require their own therapists.
3. They adhere to the self-fulfilling prophecy concept, which holds that if your child is labelled, then he will begin to act as if he actually has the disorder named because he is expected to do so.

Whatever the reason, it is common practice for parents of mentally ill children and adolescents not to know their child's diagnosis. This has misled many parents into seeking unscientific treatments. Some parents have used up precious lifetime insurance benefits or other savings in the hope of finding a quick cure. If they had been told about the illness, common forms of treatment, and the possible course of the illness, they might have been in a position to make better choices for the family as a whole.

## Budgeting Your Resources

Often parents have sacrificed the college educations of other children or have used money needed for other members' medical expenses in order to pay the psychiatric expenses for their "emotionally disturbed" child, not realizing that in reality they are facing a long-term illness for which they should budget their resources.

Although effective treatments exist for the schizophrenias, the affective disorders, and many of the other mental disorders, the family lifestyle is usually altered as a result of these recurrent mental illnesses. Families have found it wise to plan and adapt to the times when the psychosis or symptoms affecting their child may return.

## Where To Go For Help

If your child has an long-term illness, you will need to find a family support group. The best way to find a group like this is to contact the Alliance for the Mentally Ill or your local mental health clinic, and they can put you in touch with a group in your area. These groups are composed mainly of families who have a relative with long-term mental illness. They have already travelled many miles on the same road you will be travelling and they can be an invaluable guide for you. They know the good physicians, the good agencies, and can save you a great deal of time and money in your search for useful resources.

## When To Start Long-Term Planning

If your child has been diagnosed by his psychiatrist as having a long-term illness, begin to learn about federal, state, and local resources. Many families have found it wise to insist that their teenager learn some marketable skill through the vocational education program in high school while he is still covered under Public Law 94–142.

Many adolescents with a mental illness do not go on to college. However, some do, and their families have often found it more sensible to have them attend a local community college where they are close to their support system and where they can get academic help. As mentioned earlier, you might get better results if you encourage your child to take only one or two courses at a time and not overload himself.

## What Will This Illness Mean To Your Child

Many families have found it helpful to share information with their child as they learn about mental illness. It is a delicate line and you must decide for yourself when and how to help your child with the educational process. A good professional should be able to explain the illness to your child in a scientific and sensitive way. The earlier your child learns that this is an illness that affects his brain and accepts this as an illness, the earlier he can begin to move forward. Unfortunately, there are professionals who will not be honest with their patients or the families involved and persist in calling manic depression or schizophrenia "adjustment disorders" or other misleading terms. A person with a long-term mental illness will have to accept the fact that he has an illness; that it may be long-term; that there are strengths he has and that there are ways in which to offset the fact that his illness is disabling. Just as children with a defective limb must learn about the ways in which they must adjust their lives to their handicap, so must children with brain disorders learn about managing their illness.

A long-term mental illness will probably mean a change in goals for your child. Instead of aiming for a law degree, he may have the goal of living in the community, learning a skill, and maximizing the periods when he is able to work.

Acceptance of the fact of mental illness means acceptance of the treatment. Just as persons with diabetes must learn to take insulin for the rest of their lives, so many persons with severe mental illness must learn to take the medications which will diminish the delusions and hallucinations of schizophrenia, or the devastating mood swings of manic depression. It is important that you and your mentally ill child learn all you can about the medications and their side effects.

A peer group for your child may be helpful in motivating him to stay with his treatment. Some groups have developed their own client-run "drop in" centers. These centers can be very helpful in alleviating loneliness and promoting socialization after people have been discharged. There is a risk with a few peer groups that you should be aware of: some argue militantly against medication and may influence your child against his own best interests.

## What Will You Need To Do As Parents?

One of the best things you can do is learn all you can about your child's illness—the research, local resources, coping and management techniques, medications and their side effects, and how to advocate for better services and more research.

Learning about the Community Support System concept will be very helpful to you in understanding the needs of an adult with mental illness. Someday your child will be an adult and the more services available to her, the better. The Community Support Program (CSS) is a small project within the National Institute of Mental Health that has funded many demonstration programs throughout the United States for severely mentally ill persons. The CSS concept was designed by NIMH and is defined by Beth Stroul as "an organized network of caring and responsible people committed to assisting a vulnerable population meet their needs and develop their potentials without being unnecessarily isolated or excluded from the community."

The concept recognizes that the traditional mental health services are not enough and includes ten essential components to a program that provides adequate opportunities and services for persons with long-term mental illness. Stroul writes that the CSS concept calls for each community to perform the following ten functions:

1. **Location of Clients/Outreach.** Locate clients, reach out to inform them of available services and assure their access to needed services and community resources by arranging for transportation, if necessary, or by taking the services to the clients.

2. **Assistance in Meeting Basic Human Needs.** Help clients meet basic human needs for food, clothing, shelter, personal safety, general medical and dental care, and assist them in applying for income, medical, housing and other benefits which they may need and to which they are entitled.

3. **Mental Health Care.** Provide adequate mental health care including diagnostic evaluation; prescription, periodic review, and regulation of psychotropic drugs as needed; and community-based psychiatric, psychological and/or counseling and treatment services.

4. **24-Hour Crisis Assistance.** Provide 24-hour, quick response, crisis assistance to enable both the client and involved family and friends to cope with emergencies while maintaining the client's status as a functioning community member to the greatest possible extent.

5. **Psychosocial and Vocational Services.** Provide comprehensive psychosocial services which include a continuum of high to low expectation services and environments designed to improve or maintain clients' abilities to function in normal social roles. Some of these services should be available on for an indefinite period of time and should include services that train clients in daily and community living skills; help clients develop social skills, interests and leisure time activities; and help clients find and make use of appropriate employment opportunities and vocational services.

6. **Rehabilitative and Supportive Housing.** Provide a range of rehabilitative and supportive housing options for persons not in crisis who need a special living arrangement. The choices should be broad enough to allow each client an op-

portunity to live in an atmosphere offering the degree of support necessary, while also providing incentives and encouragement for clients to assume increasing responsibility for their lives.

7. **Assistance/Consultation and Education.** Provide back-up support, assistance, consultation and education to families, friends, landlords, employers, community agencies, and others who come in frequent contact with clients to maximize benefits and minimize the problems associated with the presence of these persons in the community.

8. **Natural Support Systems.** Recognize and involve natural support systems such as family self-help groups, consumer-run service alternatives, neighborhood networks, churches, community organizations, commerce, and industry.

9. **Grievance Procedures/Protection of Client Rights.** Establish grievance procedures and mechanisms to protect client rights both in and outside of mental health or residential facilities.

10. **Case Management.** Facilitate effective use by clients of helping systems by designating a single person or team responsible for helping the client to make informed choices about opportunities and services, assuring timely access to needed assistance, providing opportunities and encouragement for self-help activities, and coordinating all services to meet the client's goals.

The CSS believes that services should respect the dignity and individual needs of each person. It is based on creating opportunities for persons with mental illnesses and helping them move toward independence.

These are goals that most parent advocates work toward and are goals that you may want to keep in mind for your child as she becomes an adult. See what is available in your community, and then see what you can do to get more and better services, always aiming for the implementation of that final ten-point program.

## Developing A Long-Term Plan

As in any long-term plan, you must take into consideration all of the players involved. Too many families have plunged headlong into the care and treatment of the ill family member, not leaving any time, money, or energy for the rest of the family. Step back and look at all the aspects of planning for your family and its future in as realistic a way as possible. Ask yourself the following questions:

1. What are the possible needs of the rest of your family? Do your other children have college in their futures? What about a job change for one of the wage earners? Trips, medical and dental expenses, retirement, care of elderly family members? How much money can you realistically earn in a lifetime?
2. Can your mentally ill child live at home or should you look for supportive housing in the community?
3. What do you need to learn about coping?
4. Are there public benefits that can help financially? What are they?
5. How much should you get involved in the day-to-day case management of your child? How much is good for you and how much is good for your child and the rest of the family?
6. How long will you be able to care for your child? How can you ensure a support system for your child after your death?

When answering these questions, here are some things for you to keep in mind.

## Flexibility

It is impossible to predict all the variables that may change a well thought out plan of action for families of children with mental illness. These families learn to "hang loose," as the very nature of the illnesses— unpredictability, unreliability in following a treatment plan, inaccessibility of community resources—demands flexibility. However, it is necessary for you to keep in mind the needs of your whole family. Once you learn that there is no quick cure for severe mental illness, you can get on with a realistic plan for your family.

## Housing

Early on, you will need to decide how long you will be able to keep your mentally ill child in your home. Some families are able to do this for a number of years. In many families, the toll on parents and other siblings is too great. Also, many persons with mental illness may be able to learn independent living skills somewhat faster in community living arrangements—just as that perennially sloppy son suddenly becomes Mr. Clean when he joins the Army.

However, the living arrangements of the youth should consider the views of all family members with the final decision being made by you. You must be prepared to face the possibility that if you choose to keep your child at home, the treatment team may actively attempt to intervene and urge you to reconsider. Many professionals subscribe to the notion that it is best to separate the youngster from his family and some have gone to unusual lengths to "rescue" the child. Such professionals often view the family as part of the problem.

In many communities, there is no place for your child and you have no choice but to keep her at home. That is why families have banded together and are advocating hard for new monies to provide supportive housing, and other elements of comprehensive community support systems for their relatives.

You have to look practically at the impact on your family of having your mentally ill child live with you. Many times it works out well. In other instances, it is better for all of you to have your child elsewhere. There are few, if any, alternative arrangements for children, but there is some supportive housing for adolescents. You can find out what is available and how to get on a waiting list by contacting your local AMI office.

## Coping in the Home

There have been several excellent books written on this subject and they are listed in the Reading List. AMI groups run coping skills courses and the mental health clinics in your area may run "Coping Skills Courses." I urge you to contact either AMI or your local clinic and find out more about these courses. They are aimed toward providing you with common-sense guidelines for managing your household with your child in your home.

Holidays can be particularly stressful times for your child. She may need more quiet time away from the bustle of your family activities. If she goes to her room, it may be a signal that she needs time to regroup. Accept these retreats as a natural way to cope with an exciting, stimulating world. Even if this temporary withdrawal happens in the middle of Thanksgiving dinner, you may find that "hanging loose" is the best thing to do. Sometimes visiting with one or two people who are special to your youngster may make the occasion just enough of a celebration without overdoing it. Keeping stress levels down and having a low-keyed atmosphere can be difficult, particularly at holiday time, but the payoff can be great.

## Public Benefits

Although the role of the federal government in helping disabled persons has diminished considerably in the past ten years, and some federal functions have shifted to the states, nonetheless, there are still certain important federal benefits to which your child is entitled. *A Pocket Guide to Federal Help for the Disabled Person* is a handy introduction to the federal benefits that your taxes make possible for your child.

One program with which you are already familiar is the Education for All Handicapped Children Act (Public Law 94–142). Another program which is administered by the state departments of education is the Federal Vocational Rehabilitation Program. The services offered vary from state to state, but generally evaluation, counseling, placement, and follow-up are offered without cost. Applicants must have a "reasonable chance" of being employable following rehabilitation. Employment is defined to include sheltered workshops, activity centers, homebound work, or homemaking.

If your child is in high school, it is time to contact the Vocational Rehabilitation Agency. Together with the school, your adolescent, and the vocational rehabilitation counselor, you can develop a strong program to assist your child in getting some training that may be of use to her as an adult.

In the past, it has been very difficult to get some vocational rehabilitation programs interested in serving people with mental illness. Many programs are geared to serving mentally retarded and physically handicapped persons and have not adequately planned or trained to serve persons with mental illness, even though they are mandated to serve the mentally ill population as well as those with physical handicaps.

As you can imagine, a job can be wonderfully therapeutic for your teenager. Therefore, you must be persistent in finding what these programs offer, in asking for your child's rights as guaranteed under law, and in documenting all you have gone through in your attempts to help your child become employed. Keep a written record of all your phone calls and visits, and copies of all correspondence with the program involved. From time to time, send copies to the program director. Hopefully, this will get his attention and your child will be given increased access to the program she needs.

You will also need to keep a records folder with your child's school history and records, medical history, and psychologist's or psychiatrist's reports that document her disability (including a statement of permission for your doctor to release information and records).

## Financial Assistance

Two important federal programs provide financial assistance to disabled persons. These two programs are Social Security Disability Insurance Benefits and Supplemental Security Income. Information about these programs can be obtained from the many Social Security Administration leaflets available from your nearest Social Security Administration office.

When a disabled worker's earnings are lost or reduced due to the worker's disability, he is entitled to receive Social Security Disability Insurance benefits. Disabled workers must have credit for certain amounts of work under social security before the worker and his family can get benefits. Obviously this only has relevance to you if your teenager has been part of the work force in the past, but it is important to keep in mind when urging her to learn a trade for future work opportunities.

Supplemental Security Income (SSI) makes monthly payments to disabled, aged, and blind people who have little or no income and resources. According to the Pocket Guide, "A person is considered disabled if he has a physical or mental impairment which:

1. prevents him from working, and
2. is expected to last at least twelve months or result in death."

Your child does not need any Social Security work credits to get SSI payments. She can be eligible even if she has never worked. It is also possible to work part time and receive SSI payments. Recent changes in the Social Security regulations make it possible for SSI recipients to work some hours without losing their benefits, *including* Medicaid. This is an important change and one you may want to take advantage of if your child is able to work.

## Medical Assistance

Medicare and Medicaid are the primary sources of federal medical assistance for disabled persons.

Medicare is the health insurance program designed to serve everyone over sixty-five years of age and disabled persons under sixty-five who are entitled to receive Social Security *disability* benefits for a designated period of time.

Medicaid is a state/federal program providing health care services to persons with low incomes. Disabled persons could be eligible for Medicaid based on their income. Eligibility requirements differ from state to state, but generally persons who are receiving SSI or other public assistance may be eligible.

For more information, contact your local Social Security office, or write:

> Health Care Financing Administration;
> Inquiries Branch
> Room 1–P–4
> East Lowrise Building
> Baltimore, MD 21207

## Housing Assistance

If yours is a low income family, your child may be eligible for housing assistance payments from the U.S. Department of Housing and Urban Development (HUD). Some state and county governments have additional rental assistance for disabled persons. You can find out about your eligibility by contacting your local jurisdiction's social services office.

## Tax Benefits

The Internal Revenue Service allows many medical and dental expenses to be deducted from the income of a disabled person or his parents' income. For children with mental illness, this may include payments to a special school if the main reason for attendance is the institution's capability for "alleviating the handicap." Organizations such as the Association for Retarded Citizens, AMI or the Mental Health Association in your area may write annual booklets such as "Fact Sheets on 1986 Federal Income Tax Deductions for Handicapped Persons."

### Local and State Resources

In some areas, counties and states contribute to housing benefits, general public assistance, and job opportunities for disabled persons. Check with your local jurisdiction to see what is available for you.

## Plan

"What happens to our child when we are gone?" This is the question that haunts most parents of disabled children. Families in a growing number of areas of the country have formed organizations called PLAN (Planned Lifetime Assistance Network). For more information, contact PLAN directly. It is a good idea to also check with a lawyer who is familiar with the laws pertaining to handicapped persons. AMI also has some basic literature that might help you.

### Estates, Trusts, and Wills

Another important consideration for "What will happen after I'm gone?" is the setting up of trusts and wills. The proceeds of wills and trusts can be paid to the various PLANs for the benefit of your child. In order for this to be done, consult a lawyer or someone who is knowledgeable about the federal and state laws affecting disabled people. Some parents make the mistake of leaving their estate to their disabled child. The entire estate could be wiped out with a single hospitalization, leaving nothing for your child's future. Trusts must contain strong spendthrift trust provisions and must not be within the control of your child. It is important that your child receive government benefits such as SSI and Medicaid, and your trust must be set up so that the trustees will be able to use the monies for the benefit of your child without jeopardizing his government benefits. An excellent booklet describing setting up wills and trusts is written by the Association for Retarded Citizens, and you can get a copy from them.

## From Parent to Parent

This is a chapter about planning—of thinking ahead when you know or suspect that your child has a long-term mental illness. Your dreams have changed, your hopes are grounded in more realistic planning, your whole family has learned a great deal about mental illness.

Take one day at a time. Be good to yourselves, learn from other parents, keep on learning. Demand changes in systems for your child so that there are more and better services available to her and advocate for more research in the brain so that someday we will know the causes, and then the cures, for long-term mental illnesses.

## REFERENCES

American Psychiatric Association. *Diagnostic and Statistical Manual of Mental Disorders.* 3d ed., rev. Washington, D.C.: American Psychiatric Association (1400 K St. NW, Washington, DC 20005), 1987.

American Psychiatric Association. *Psychiatric Glossary.* Washington, D.C.: American Psychiatric Association Press, 1984.

Andreasen, N.C., M.D., Ph.D. *The Broken Brain.* New York: Harper and Row, 1984.

Association for Retarded Citizens. *How to Provide for Their Future.* Arlington, TX: Association for Retarded Citizens (National Headquarters, PO Box 6109, Arlington, TX 76011), 1984.

Harding, C.M., J. Zubin, and J.S. Strauss. "Chronicity in Schizophrenia: Fact, Partial Fact, or Artifact?" *Hospital and Community Psychiatry* 38, no. 5 (May, 1987): 477–86.

Hatfield, Agnes. *Consumer Guide to Mental Health Services.* Arlington, VA: National Alliance for the Mentally Ill (1901 N. Fort Myer Drive, #500, Arlington, VA 22209), 1985.

Hatfield, Agnes. *Coping With Mental Illness in the Family: A Family Guide.* Baltimore: Dept. of Health and Mental Hygiene, 1984. Can be purchased at the National Alliance for the Mentally Ill, 1901 N. Fort Myer Drive, #500, Arlington, VA 22209.

Kanter, Joel S. *Coping Strategies for Relatives of the Mentally Ill.* Arlington, VA: National Alliance for the Mentally Ill. 1982.

National Alliance for the Mentally Ill. *Reading List and Resource List.*

Office of Information and Resources for the Handicapped, U.S. Department of Education; *Pocket Guide to Federal help for the Disabled Person,* Washington, D.C., 1985.

Papolos, Demitri, F., M.D. and Janice Papolos. *Overcoming Depression.* New York: Harper and Row, 1987.

Rosenthal, R., and L. Jacobson. *Pygmalion in the Classroom.* New York: Holt, Rinehart & Winston, 1968.

Russell, Mark *Alternatives: A Family Guide to Legal and Financial Planning for the Disabled.* Evanston: First Publications, 1983. Available from National Alliance for the Mentally Ill.

Stroul, Beth. *Models of Community Support Services: Approaches to Helping Persons With Long Term Mental Illness.* National Institute of Mental Health Community Support Program, August, 1986. Available from Center for Psychiatric Rehabilitation, Sargent College of Allied Health Professions, Boston University, 1019 Commonwealth Ave., Boston, MA 02215.

Terkeleson, Kenneth, M.D. Schizophrenia and the Family: Adverse Effects of Family Therapy. *Family Process* 22 (1983): 191–200.

Torrey, E. Fuller, M.D. *Surviving Schizophrenia: A Family Manual.* New York: Harper and Row, 1983.

# Parent Statements

We never dreamed that Kim would be sick for a long time. We were told, finally, about her mental illness but we assumed she would get some therapy and be fine. It was a terrible blow to realize that we would have to take care of her for the rest of her life. The most we can hope for is that she will be well enough to work part of the time and help out, but we don't think she'll ever be totally on her own.

≡❈≡

Jerry was the "problem" child. He was the one we had to take care of all the time. He got the special doctors, the expensive therapists, everything. Luke was always left on the sidelines. He was okay so we just sort of forgot about him. Now Luke's grown and he's just sort of forgotten about us, too.

≡❈≡

My sixteen-year-old daughter has schizophrenia. What I keep asking is, "Does anyone ever get over it?"

≡❈≡

It's so hard to get your hopes up every time he seems better just to have them dissolved by another episode. It's too hard to cope with. We're not getting any younger and it's harder and harder to bounce back. Now we try not to expect any change, then we're not so likely to be disappointed.

≡❈≡

We went to a lawyer to make sure that George would be taken care of after we're dead. It's just not fair to ask his sister to take the responsibility.

≡❈≡

The worst thing is to try to adjust to the idea that all your hopes are gone and so is the kid you loved so much. Instead, you're faced with this burden, maybe for the rest of your lives.

≡❈≡

Carole wasn't able to handle college. So we enrolled her in a vocational program. Luckily it's a pretty good one. She's working now on becoming a secretary. She can't be a full-time employee but she can work at one of those temporary places. She feels good about herself and is even planning around the times when she can't function.

No one would give us a concrete diagnosis. By the time we finally found out what was wrong, she was too old for most of the programs through school. We're on our own.

Sidney has schizophrenia. He's almost grown now and I keep hoping that he'll get better but I don't see any signs yet.

Alice can never live at home. It's just that simple. She takes over our lives. We've had too many years of it and now we want a little quiet. I have her name on every halfway house list in three states. We don't mind driving to see her, no matter how far, but we want to come home and be able to relax. I guess that makes us bad parents, but that's what we want anyhow.

We had such high hopes for Alex. He was so bright and cheerful. We expected him to be a doctor or an astronaut—somebody really special. Then he got depression. He's one of those that can't take Lithium and the other drugs are harder to work with. He spends so much time just coping that there's not enough left over to do much.

# Appendix A
=✾=

# Medications

This appendix is designed to give you additional information on the drugs your child may be taking. It can only be a general guide for you to use as a reference. You will need to get more information on the specific medications your child is taking from his physician.

## Remember These Points:

1. Tell your physician that you want to be educated about what kind of behavior to expect from your child when the medication is started, what signs of problems you should watch for, and who to call if something unusual happens that you think is linked to the medication.
2. Adults should supervise children's medication.
3. Each doctor should be informed about the medications others have prescribed.
4. A physician should monitor the child's medication use and see that proper laboratory or other testing is completed when necessary.
5. Children should have professional and family support while on medication.
6. Older children should be educated about their medication by experts.
7. Regular checkups and assessments need to be performed for children receiving psychoactive medication.

# Know:

1. When your child should take his medication.
2. How your child should take it.
3. What foods or drinks to avoid.
4. What activities to avoid while on the medication.
5. What the possible side effects are.
6. Your doctor's phone number and report any action that you think may be a side effect. Be assertive with your doctor. He is there to help you.
7. Make sure you understand all instructions about the medication.

# Psychiatric Medications
## Antipsychotics (Major Tranquilizers)

These medications are used for children and adults with serious disorders, characterized by aggressiveness, anxiety, or psychosis. Sometimes these drugs are referred to as neuroleptics.

| Generic Name | Trade Name | Generic Name | Trade Name |
|---|---|---|---|
| **Phenothiazines:** | | | Thiorill |
| Acetophenazine | Tindal | Trifluoperazine | Stelazine |
| Chlorpromazine | Thorazine | | Clinazine |
| | Chloramead | | Novoflurazine |
| | Chlorprom | | Pentazine |
| | ChlorPromanyl | | Solazine |
| | Largactil | | Terfluzine |
| | Promachlor | | Triflurin |
| | Promapar | | Tripazine |
| | Promosol | Triflupromazine | Vesprin |
| | Terpium | | |
| | Sonazine | **Other Antipsychotic Medications:** | |
| Fluphenazine | Prolixin | | |
| | Permitil | Haloperidol | Haldol |
| Mesoridazine | Serentil | Chlorprothixene | Taractan |
| Perphenazine | Trilafon | Thiothixene | Navane |
| Promazine | Sparine | Loxapine | Loxitane |
| Thioridazine | Mellaril | Molindone | Moban |
| | Novoridazine | | |

Acute psychotic conditions, including the schizophrenias, may improve rapidly when treated with these drugs, but chronic schizophrenia may require three weeks or more of use before improvement is seen.

Treatment with more than one antipsychotic medication at the same time is rarely indicated.

**Frequent Side Effects:** drowsiness, low blood pressure, dryness of the mouth, possible constipation, and rapid pulse rate. Some people gain weight. Blurred vision for reading, not usually a problem for long-range vision. Rashes can occur. May appear to move slower than usual. Can cause some bodily swelling, and menstrual irregularities.

**Occasional Side Effects:** Parkinson-like symptoms: zombie look, drooling, tremors, muscular rigidity, and muscle fatigue and weakness. Other side effects include spasms of tongue, jaw, eyes and neck, rotation of the eyeballs, a tight feeling in the throat, or assuming bizarre positions. Some men complain of difficulty with ejaculation, specifically if thioridazine (Mellaril) is used.

Some of the medications reduce sexual urges. They can cause the secretion of milk from the breasts, and women have tested positive on pregnancy tests when not actually pregnant (false positives).

**Rare Side Effects:** Jaundice (a yellow or orange colored skin), bone marrow suppression, fever, and seizures with high doses. "Neuroleptic Malignant Syndrome," a serious cluster of adverse effects of the medication which usually involves a high fever, muscular rigidity, and alteration in level of consciousness, can result in a coma and changes in the nervous system that affect blood pressure, heart rate, and breathing.

**Report to the doctor:**

| | |
|---|---|
| skin rash | weakness or tremors |
| sore throat | muscle spasms anywhere |
| dark-colored urine | any interference with voluntary |
| jaundice | muscle movement |
| pale stools | muscle rigidity (stiffness) |
| fever | visual changes |

**Precautions:**
Your child may have difficulty adjusting to extremes in temperatures. Avoid having him use electric heating pads or hot water bottles, since he may not be able to judge temperature well.

His eyes may be sensitive to bright light. If necessary, have him wear sunglasses when outside.

Protect his skin from the sun.

Make sure he drinks enough fluids.

Tell your doctor about *all the medications he is taking,* including allergy and cold pills sold over-the-counter. Alcohol or street drugs will significantly alter the effects of his prescribed medications.

Make sure your child has regular dental checkups.

Use caution with children who have seizure disorders.

**Tardive Dyskinesia,** a term used to describe a set of abnormal, involuntary movements, is a possible side effect of most of the major antipsychotic medications. It is characterized in part by involuntary movements, particularly of the lips and tongue, but sometimes of the fingers, toes, or trunk. Long term studies have suggested that 15 to 20 percent of the patients taking antipsychotic drugs for several years may develop this condition. The symptoms may become apparent after the medication is withdrawn. Persons with affective disorders and those who are mentally retarded seem especially vulnerable to developing this disorder when they take these drugs. It is probably best avoided by limiting the dosage and duration of use of antipsychotic drugs. A new medication (Clozapine) is *thought* to reduce the incidence of tardive dyskinesia because it acts on different receptor sites in the brain than most other major tranquilizers. It is, however, *experimental* at this point.

## *Antidepressants*

Intense, long lasting depression which does not resolve spontaneously or by psychotherapy alone requires treatment with medications. This is especially true for persons who develop difficulty in sleeping, as well as changes in appetite, weight, and menstrual periods. Some physicians selectively prescribe them for persons suffering from severe pain.

| Generic Name | Trade Name | Generic Name | Trade Name |
|---|---|---|---|
| **Tricyclic:** | | Imipramine | Tofranil |
| Amitriptyline | Elavil | | Janimine |
| | Endep | | Presamine |
| | Amitid | | SK- Pramine |
| | Amitril | Imipramine | |
| | Sk Amitriptyline | pamoate | Tofranil-PM |
| Amoxapine | Asendin | Nortriptyline | Aventyl |
| Desipramine | Norpramin | | Pamelor |
| | Pentofrane | Protriptyline | Vivactil |
| Doxepin | Sinequan | Trimipramine | Surmontil |
| | Adapin | | |

It takes about one to three weeks of use before the antidepressant effects occur. Your doctor might wish to order blood tests to insure that the medicine is given in adequate does to reach "therapeutic levels."

**Common Side Effects:** drowsiness, blurred vision, constipation, urinary hesitancy, dry mouth, rash, and lightheadedness upon arising. These signs often pass with continued use.

**Occasional Side Effects:** Effects on the heart rate and irregular heart rhythms and blood pressure have been noted. Blood changes can occur and periodic blood tests need to be routinely done. Glaucoma can be aggravated by these medicines.

**Report to the doctor:**

drowsiness
drop or rise in temperature
rapid pulse rate
palpitations or arythmia
  (irregular heartbeat)

change in level of consciousness
agitation
hyperactive reflexes
muscle rigidity
vomiting

**Precautions:**Your teenager's ability to drive an automobile or perform other potentially hazardous activities may be impaired.

His response to alcohol, barbiturates and other depressants may be enhanced.

*Persons with manic depressive illness may become manic or hypomanic with antidepressants.* Individualized care by a physician is required.

If your child abruptly discontinues his medication, medical problems may result.

These medicines must be used with caution in persons with seizure disorders.

## Other Antidepressants: Monoamine Oxidase Inhibitors (MAOI)

MAOI inhibit the enzyme which catabolizes the neurotransmitters such as Dopamine and Norepinephrine. Thus, as the breakdown (metabolism) slows down, the neurotransmitter concentrations increase. Considering that depressions are due to decreasing of the neurotransmitters, these medications provide a direct effect to reverse such decreases and increase neurotransmitters.

| Generic Name | Trade Name | Generic Name | Trade Name |
|---|---|---|---|
| Isocarboxazid | Marplan | Tranylcypromine | Parnate |
| Phenelzine | Nardil | | |

**Common Side Effects:** Dry mouth, blurred vision, rash, appetite loss, low blood pressure upon rising, disturbances in heart rate and rhythm. Dizziness, headache, overactivity, tremors and, rarely, weight gain.

**Occasional Side Effects:** Nervousness, confusion, memory impairment, insomnia, weakness and fatigue, constipation, nausea, and diarrhea.

**Risks:** Dietary restrictions accompany the use of this medication. Foods and beverages with a high concentration of tyramine (cheese, beer, wine, pickled herring, chicken liver, yeast extract) should be avoided. Other foods may also cause problems. Check with your doctor for a list. There may be a high blood pressure crisis. This crisis may be preceded by palpitations or frequent headaches, nausea, dizziness, sweating, or chest pain. *Avoid any over-the-counter drugs* without checking first with your doctor.

**Report to the doctor:**

| | |
|---|---|
| Jaundiced skin color | severe frontal headaches, |
| blurred vision | pallor, chest pain |
| abdominal distention | chills, sweats |
| rapid heart rate | seizures |
| inability to urinate | poor coordination |
| extreme excitement | swelling of the throat (thyroid |
| psychosis aggravated | gland) |

**Note:** Because of the strict dietary restrictions necessary with these medications, a rather high level of motivation and commitment from the patient is necessary when prescribing these drugs. You will have to determine if your child is ready for the responsibility involved in following this medication plan. Because substance abusers and young children are often unreliable, they are poor candidates for these drugs.

## Other Mood Regulators:

| Generic Name | Trade Name | Generic Name | Trade Name |
|---|---|---|---|
| Lithium | Eskalith | | Lithobid |
| Carbonate | Lithane | Lithium Citrate | Cibalith-S |

Lithium is effective in controlling emotional or mental conditions that show a wide mood swing. These conditions are referred to as manic-depressive illnesses, major affective disorders, or bipolar affective disorders. Lithium can be effective within three to four days, especially for the manic patient. Not everyone responds to the drug.

## Common Side Effects:

increased thirst
increased urination
feeling slightly ill or
   nauseated
mild stomach cramps
shakiness of the hands
mild sleepiness
slight muscular weakness

decreased sexual ability or
   interest
occasional loose stools
weight gain
metallic taste
dry mouth
worsening of acne or psoriasis

## Occasionally after prolonged use the following may occur:

Changes in the kidney and thyroid functioning. Laboratory tests need to be routinely done to assess these areas. Changes in white blood cell count may also occur and blood tests need to be completed periodically. Changes in heart rhythms and brain wave patterns have occasionally been noted.

## Report to the doctor:

pregnancy
persistent diarrhea
vomiting or severe nausea
coarse trembling of hands or
   legs
frequent muscle twitching
blurred vision
confusion

weakness
extreme dizziness
slurred speech
irregular heart beat
swelling of the feet or legs
other change in behavior that
   is unusual

Therapeutic blood levels should be done periodically to insure that the amount of Lithium in the blood is within the "therapeutic range." Laboratory tests to determine the kidney, liver, and thyroid functioning must be done regularly.

**Note:** Lithium may be harmful to unborn babies. Always inform your doctor of all types of medication your child is taking. Ask his or her advice before giving your child any over-the-counter drug. Some experts have described reversible brain damage occurring with some persons who received both lithium carbonate and haloperidol together at high dosages. Close monitoring of persons receiving these drug combinations is required. The effectiveness of lithium for treating children with mood swings has not been established.

## Other Mood Regulators (continued):

| Generic Name | Trade Name |
|---|---|
| Carbamazepine | Tegretol |

This drug is actually an anticonvulsant medication that has been found to be effective with some types of bipolar affective disorders. It appears to have an antimanic effect in some persons. It has been used for individuals who have temporal lobe epilepsy as well. It is one of the medications used to treat persons who can no longer take Lithium. Experts have noted that Lithium and tegretol in combination may result in positive results when neither of the drugs alone produced those findings. Some persons who have four or more episodes of mania per year have been reported to respond well to this combination of medications. In general, it is not as effective as Lithium.

**Common Side Effects:** Mild to moderate dizziness when first taken. Slight nausea may occur.

**Occasional Side Effects:** Bone marrow depression, serious anemias, and other blood changes. Close monitoring of blood, urine, liver, and kidney function tests are required.

**Report to the doctor:**

| | |
|---|---|
| persistent dizziness | diarrhea |
| drowsiness | loss of appetite |
| difficulty walking straight | difficulty urinating |
| blurred vision | impotence |
| double vision | skin rashes |
| vomiting | excessive sweating |
| abdominal pain | fever, chills |

## Precautions:

Have your child avoid activities that require alertness and good psychomotor coordination until his response to the drug has been determined. Make sure he has his blood tested periodically.

**Note:** Some experts claim that the effectiveness of oral contraceptives is reduced when tegretol is taken; thus, possibly contributing to unwanted pregnancies.

## AntiParkinsonian Medications

| Generic Name | Trade Name | Generic Name | Trade Name |
|---|---|---|---|
| Amantadine | Symmetrel | Diphenhydramine | Benedryl |
| Benztropine | Cogentin | Procyclidine | Kemadrin |
| Biperidin | Akineton | Trihexyphenidyl | Artane |

These drugs are often given to counteract the side effects of the antipsychotic medications.

**Common Side Effects:** blurred vision, restlessness, dry mouth, and constipation.

**Occasional Side Effects:** rapid pulse rate, palpitations, abdominal problems, vomiting, and toxic psychosis.

**Report to the Doctor:**
incoherence
hallucinations
headache
sedation
depression

muscular weakness
palpitations, rapid or periodic
  slow heart rate
vomiting
urinary retention

**Precautions:**
Have your child avoid activities requiring alertness until he is used to the drug.

Check the amount of his urinary output to make sure it is normal.

Have him take his medication after meals to prevent stomach irritation.

He must never abruptly stop taking this drug. Do not use if glaucoma is present.

## *Hypnosedatives (Minor Tranquilizers)*

These medications are used to relieve anxiety (nervousness and tension) that results from distressing situations. Several also are used to treat sleeplessness; others relieve muscle spasm. They are also used as anticonvulsive medications to control epilepsy.

### Benzodiazepines (Short Acting)

| Generic Name | Trade Name | Generic Name | Trade Name |
|---|---|---|---|
| Alprazolam | Xanax | Temazepam | Restoril |
| Lorazepam | Ativan | Triazolam | Halcion |
| Oxazepam | Serax | | |

### Benzodiazepines (Long Acting)

| Generic Name | Trade Name | Generic Name | Trade Name |
|---|---|---|---|
| Chlordiazepoxide | Librium | Flurazepam | Dalmane |
| Clorazepate | Tranxene | Prazepam | Centrax |
| Diazepam | Valium | | |

**Side Effects:** sores or ulcers in the mouth or throat, hallucinations, mental confusion, or depression.

**Report to the doctor:**

skin rash
itching
sore throat or fever
unusual excitement
difficulty sleeping
irritability
changes in vision, especially
   blurriness

clumsiness
slurred speech
stomach pain
vomiting
diarrhea, nausea
difficulty in urination
drowsiness, headache
weakness

**Precautions:**

Check with your doctor before letting your child take any depressants, such as alcohol, sleep aids, and cold remedies. These medications will add to the depressant qualities of the other drugs and slow down his nervous system. Gradually reducing the amount of the medication is necessary before stopping completely. Some experts recommend *against* daytime administration of these drugs since they can make the mental confusion worse. These medications are addictive.

## Barbiturates (Sleeping Pills)

| Generic Name | Trade Name | Generic Name | Trade Name |
|---|---|---|---|
| Amobarbital | Amytal | Secobarbital with | |
| Pentobarbital | Nembutal | Amobarbital | Tuinal |
| Phenobarbital | Luminal | | |

These are usually prescribed as sedatives. Phenobarbital is also used for seizure control.

**Side effects:** Excessive sleepiness.

**Precautions:**
If withdrawn abruptly, your child may suffer convulsions. These medicines are addictive; therefore, your doctor should closely supervise the use *and* discontinuation.

## Stimulants

| Generic Name | Trade Name | Generic Name | Trade Name |
|---|---|---|---|
| Methylphenidate | Ritalin | Magnesium | |
| Dextroamphet- | | pemoline | Cylert |
| amine | Dexedrine | | |

These drugs are often prescribed for children who suffer from attention deficit disorder with or without hyperactivity. They appear to calm youngsters. Ritalin and Cylert would not be used with children under the age of six. Dexedrine is used infrequently now due to its higher addictive potential. One must use caution with children who have seizure disorders.

**Side Effects:**

anorexia

irritability headache

variable blood pressure
response

heart changes

occasionally will overstimulate

weight loss

abdominal pain

**Note:** Cylert has been cited by some as causing liver problems. All stimulants cause occasional mood swings.

## REFERENCES

Abramowicz, M., ed. *The Medical Letter on Drugs and Therapeutics,* October 22, 1976. 56 Harrison Street, New Rochelle, NY 10801.

Biederman, J. and M. Jellinek. "Current Concepts: Psychopharmacology in Children." *The New England Journal of Medicine* 310, no. 15 (April 12, 1984): 968–72.

D'Arcy, P.F. "Drug Interactions with Oral Contraceptives." *Drug Intelligence and Clinical Pharmacy* 20 (May 1986): 353–62.

Kane, J.M. and J.M. Smith. "Tardive Dyskinesia: Prevalence and Risk Factors, 1959–1979." *Archives of General Psychiatry* 39 (April 1982): 473–80.

Lipinski, J.F. and H.G. Pope. "Possible Synergistic Action Between Carbamazepine and Lithium Carbonate in the Treatment of Three Acutely Manic Patients." *American Journal of Psychiatry* 139, no. 7 (1982): 948–49.

Mann, S.C. et al. "Early Onset of Severe Dyskinesia Following Lithium-Haloperidol Treatment." *American Journal of Psychiatry* 140, no. 10 (October 1983): 1385–86.

Maxmen, J.S. *Essential Psychopathology.* New York: W.W. Norton & Company, 1986.

*Nursing 86 Drug Handbook.* Springhouse, Pa.: SpringhouseCorporation Book Division, 1986.

Post, R.M. and T.W. Uhde. "Carbamazepine and Lithium Carbonate Synergism in Mania." *Archives of General Psychiatry* 41 (1984): 210.

The Task Force on Late Neurological Effects of Antipsychotic Drugs (APA). *Tardive Dyskinesia: Summary of a Task Force Report of the American Psychiatric Association* 137, no. 10 (October 1980): 1163–72.

## Appendix B
=≡❧≡=

# Directory of State Organizations

This directory contains references to organizations that can help parents of children with mental illness. It is as complete as possible. There may be new groups that have formed since this book went to press. Call the national offices to get more information about the organizations in your area.

## National Offices:

National Alliance for the
  Mentally Ill
1901 N. Fort Myer Drive
Suite 500
Arlington, VA 22209
703/524–7600

National Mental Health
  Association
1021 Prince Street
Alexandria, VA 22314–2971
703/684–7722

### ALABAMA

Mental Health Association of
  Alabama
306 Whitman Street
Montgomery, AL 36104
205/834–3857

### ALASKA

Alaska Alliance for the Mentally Ill
P.O. Box 2543
Fairbanks, AK 99707
907/457–3733

Mental Health Association of Alaska
2611 Fairbanks Street
Anchorage, AK 99503
907/276–1705

## ARIZONA

Arizona Alliance for the Mentally Ill
c/o Robert Richter
2515 E. Thomas
S-16
Box 656
Phoenix, AZ 85016
602/273-0080

Mental Health Association of
   Moricopa County
1515 East Osborn Rd.
Phoenix, AZ 95014

## ARKANSAS

Arkansas Alliance for the Mentally Ill
Help and Hope Inc.
Hendrix Hall 125
4313 W. Markham
Little Rock, AR 72201

## CALIFORNIA

California Alliance for the Mentally Ill
2306 J Street
#203
Sacramento, CA 95816
916/443-6417

Mental Health Association of
   California
P.O. Box 162695
Sacramento, CA 95816
916/444-0324

## COLORADO

Colorado Alliance for the Mentally Ill
1100 Fillmore St.
Denver, CO 80206
303/321-3104

Mental Health Association of
   Colorado
1391 N. Speer Blvd.
#350
Denver, CO 80204

## CONNECTICUT

Connecticut Alliance for the
   Mentally Ill
284 Battis Rd.
Hamden, CT 06514
203/248-3351

Mental Health Association of
   Connecticut
705-A New Britain Ave.
Hartford, CT 06106
203/547-0337

## DELAWARE

Mental Health Association of
   Delaware
1813 North Franklin St.
Wilmington, DE 19802
303/656-8308

## DISTRICT OF COLUMBIA

Mental Health Association of the
   District of Columbia
1628 16th St. NW
4th Floor
Washington, DC 20005
202/265-6363

## FLORIDA

Florida Alliance for the Mentally Ill
7096 Pine Bluff Drive
Lake Worth, FL 33467
305/439-0539

Mental Health Association of Florida
345 South Magnolia, Suite A-13
Tallahassee, FL 32301
904/877-4707

## GEORGIA

Georgia Alliance for the Mentally Ill
1362 W. Peachtree St. NW
Atlanta, GA 30309
404/874-7351

Mental Health Association of
Georgia
1244 Clairmont Rd.
Suite 204
Decatur, GA 30030
404/634-2850

## HAWAII

Mental Health Association of Hawaii
200 North Vineyard Blvd. #507
Honolulu, HI 968817
808/521-1846

## IDAHO

Mental Health Association of Idaho
715 S. Capitol Blvd. Suite 401
Boise, ID 83720
208/343-4866

## ILLINOIS

Alliance for the Mentally Ill Illinois
State Coalition
PO Box 863
Glenview, IL 60025
312/729-1457

Mental Health Association of Illinois
1325 S. Arlington Heights Rd.
Suite 101
Elk Grove Village, IL 60007
312/956-0696

## INDIANA

Indiana Alliance for the Mentally Ill
Box 8186
Fort Wayne, IN 46808
219/432-4085

Mental Health Association of Indiana
1433 North Meridian St.
Indianapolis, IN 46202
317/638-3501

## IOWA

Iowa Alliance for the Mentally Ill
509 E. 30th St.
Davenport, IA 52803
319/322-5845

## KANSAS

Kansas Families for Mental Health
AMI
c/o Howard Snyder
4811 W. 77th Pl.
Prairie Village, KS 66208
913/642-4389

Mental Health Association of Kansas
1205 W. Harrison
Topeka, KS 66612

# KENTUCKY

Kentucky Alliance for the Mentally Ill
c/o Kathleen Whipple
145 Constitution Ave.
Lexington, KY 40508
606/252-5518

Mental Health Association of
Kentucky
Suite 104
310 West Liberty St.
Louisville, KY 40202
502/585-4161

# LOUISIANA

Louisiana Alliance for the Mentally Ill
1633 Letitia St.
Baton Rouge, LA 708008
504/344-2208

Mental Health Association of
Louisiana
6700 Plaza Dr.
Suite 104
New Orleans, LA 70127
504/241-3462

# MAINE

Maine State Alliance for the Mentally Ill
c/o Mal Wilson
PO Box 307
Oakland, ME 04963
207/547-3639

Mental Health Association of
Cumberland
169 Lancaster St.
Portland, ME 04101
207/772-6222

# MARYLAND

Alliance for the Mentally Ill of
Maryland, Inc.
2500 N. Charles St.
Baltimore, MD 21218
301/235-2511

Mental Health Association of
Maryland
323 East 25th St.
Baltimore, MD 21218
301/235-9786

# MASSACHUSETTS

Alliance for the Mentally Ill of
Massachusetts, Inc.
227 Mt. Hope Rd.
Somerset, MA 02726
617/367-8890

Mental Health Association of
Massachusetts
14 Beacon St.
Boston, MA 02108

# MICHIGAN

State Alliance for the Mentally Ill of
Michigan
c/o Hank Spitzig
17331 Fairfield
Livonia, MI 48152
313/421-4825

Mental Health Association of
Michigan
15920 West Twelve Mile Rd.
Southfield, MI 48076

## MINNESOTA

Mental Health Advocates
Coalition of Minnesota, Inc.
265 Fort Rd.
St. Paul, MN 55102
612/222-2741

Mental Health Association of
Minnesota
328 East Hennepin
Minneapolis, MN 55414
612/331-6840

## MISSISSIPPI

Mental Health Association of
Mississippi
1800 23rd Ave.
Meridian, MS 39301
601/485-3038

## MISSOURI

Missouri Coalition of Alliance for the
Mentally Ill
c/o Nate Raymond
10 Blackpool Lane
St. Louis, MO 63132

Mental Health Association of
Missouri
PO Box 1742
Joplin, MO 64804

## MONTANA

Mental Health Association of
Montana
555 Fuller Avenue
Helena, MT 59601-3302
406/442-4276

## NEBRASKA

Alliance for the Mentally Ill of
Nebraska
c/o Don Wilson
PO Box 31542
Omaha, NE 68131
402/493-2519

## NEW HAMPSHIRE

Alliance for the Mentally Ill in New
Hampshire
20 Cabot Dr.
Nashua, NH 03060
603/924-3069

## NEW JERSEY

New Jersey Alliance for the Mentally Ill
c/o M. Goldstein
Box 101 Hoes Lane
Piscataway, NJ 08854
201/463-4059

Mental Health Association of New
Jersey
60 South Fullerton Avenue
Montclair, NJ 07042
201/744-2500

## NEW MEXICO

Alliance for the Mentally Ill-New
Mexico
PO Box 9049
Santa Fe, NM 87504-9049
505/983-2584

## NEW YORK

Alliance for the Mentally Ill of New
York State
PO Box 746
New Paltz, NY 12561
914/255-5134

Mental Health Association of New
York State
196 Morton Avenue
Albany, NY 12202
518/449-5677

## NORTH CAROLINA

North Carolina Alliance for the
Mentally Ill
5105 Burr Oak Circle
Raleigh, NC 27612
919/781-5212

Mental Health Association of North
Carolina
5 West Hargett St.
Suite 705
Raleigh, NC 27601

## NORTH DAKOTA

Mental Health Association of North
Dakota
PO Box 1620
Bismarck, ND 58502
701/225-3692

## OHIO

Ohio Family Alliance for the
Mentally Ill
199 S. Central Ave.
Columbus, OH 43223
614/274-7000

Mental Health Association of Ohio
50 West Broad St.
Suite 2440
Columbus, OH 43215
614/221-5383

## OKLAHOMA

Oklahoma Alliance for the Mentally Ill
c/o Hollis Terry
10404 Sunrise Blvd.
Oklahoma City, OK 73120
405/751-2885

Mental Health Association of Tulsa
Suite 214-W
3314 East 51st St.
Tulsa, OK 74137
918/747-3797

## OREGON

Oregon Alliance of Advocates for
the Mentally Ill
5884 E. St.
Springfield, OR 97482

## PENNSYLVANIA

Mental Health Association of
Pennsylvania
900 Market St.
Harrisburg, PA 17101
717/273-5781

## RHODE ISLAND

Mental Health Association of Rhode
Island
89 Park St.
Providence, RI 02908
401/272-6730

## SOUTH CAROLINA

South Carolina Alliance for the
Mentally Ill
PO Box 2538
Columbia, SC 29202
803/736-1542

Mental Health Association of South
Carolina
1823 Gadsden St.
Columbia, SC 29201
803/779-5363

## TENNESSEE

Tennessee Alliance for the Mentally Ill
c/o John L. Lewis
416 E. Thompson Lane
Nashville, TN 37211
615/361-7585

Mental Health Association of
Tennessee
2416 Hillsboro Rd.
Nashville, TN 37212
615/298-1126

## TEXAS

Texas Alliance for the Mentally Ill
PO Box 50434
Austin, TX 78763
512/327-4253

Mental Health Association of Texas
1111 West 24th St.
Austin, TX 78705
512/476-0611

## UTAH

Utah Alliance for the Mentally Ill
156 Westminster Ave.
Salt Lake City, UT 84115

Mental Health Association of Utah
3760 Highland Dr.
#304
Salt Lake City, UT 84106
801/278-2889

## VERMONT

Alliance for the Mentally Ill of
Vermont
c/o Roch Thibodeaux
130 Foster Ave.
Burlington, VT 05401
802/862-0000

## VIRGINIA

Virginia Alliance for the Mentally Ill
217 Governor St.
Richmond, VA 23219
804/786-2412

Mental Health Association of
Virginia
5001 West Broad St.
Suite 34
Richmond, VA 23230
804/288-1805

## WASHINGTON

Alliance for the Mentally Ill of
Washington State
PO Box 2174
Vancouver, WA 98684
206/892-6323

## WEST VIRGINIA

Alliance for the Mentally Ill of West
Virginia
c /o Jim Ferry
PO Box 8266
Huntington, WV 25705
304/736-8181

Mental Health Association of West
Virginia
701½ Lee St. West
Charleston, WV 25301
304/340-3512

## WISCONSIN

Alliance for the Mentally Ill of
Wisconsin, Inc.
1245 E. Washington Ave.
Madison, WI 53703
608/845-6141

Mental Health Association of
Wisconsin
103 N. Hamilton
Madison, WI 53703
608/256-9041

## WYOMING

Wyoming Alliance for the Mentally Ill
c/o Marjorie Haass
1123 Beaumont Dr.
Casper, WY 82601
307/234-4775

## Appendix C
=❦=

# Other Resources

**American Bar Association, Commission on the Mentally Disabled,** 1800 M Street, NW, Washington, DC 20036. *The Mental Disability Law Reporter,* a journal, publishes case law developments and includes information on new and pending cases. Excellent publication.

**American Coalition of Citizens with Disabilities,** 1200 Fifteenth Street, NW, Washington DC 20005. Services include advocacy, information, and referral.

**Association for Children and Adults with Learning Disabilities,** 4156 Library Rd., Pittsburgh, PA 15234.

**Boston University, Center for Rehabilitation Research and Training in Mental Health.** The newsletter, *Community Support Network News,* is informative. *The Psychosocial Rehabilitation Journal* is an excellent publication that covers a wide range of topics relevant to rehabilitating the seriously mentally ill. Address is 1019 Commonwealth Ave., Boston, MA 02215.

**Child and Adolescent Services System Program (CASSP).** This is a National Institute of Mental Health (NIMH) program. Federal grants are competitively awarded to states for improving and coordinating mental health and educational services for children and adolescents with serious emotional problems. Address: CASSP Technical Assistance Center, Georgetown University Child Development Center, 3800 Reservoir Rd., NW, Washington, DC 20007.

**Children's Defense Fund.** 122 C St., NW, Washington, DC 20001. Provides information and publications on educational and health needs of handicapped youths.

**Council for Exceptional Children, Legislative Information,** 1920 Association Drive, Reston, VA 22091. CEC provides information on laws applying to the education of handicapped children and adolescents.

**Council of State Administrators of Vocational Rehabilitation.** According to Federal Law, 10 percent of Federal funds to states for vocational education must be used in programs for students with handicaps. This office can tell you how the funds are being used in your state. Address: Suite 401, 1055 Jefferson St., NW, Washington, D.C. 20007.

**Disability Rights Center,** 1346 Connecticut Avenue, NW, Washington, DC 20036. This center advocates for the rights of all disabled people by monitoring legislation, managing programs, and drafting regulations and guidelines.

**Depression and Related Affective Disorders Association (DRADA).** This group comprises professionals, consumers, and family members who have organized to educate others about the affective disorders, to promote research, to organize support groups, and to develop a center of excellence for the treatment of these disorders. The group is associated with the Johns Hopkins University, School of Medicine, Department of Psychiatry. Address is Meyer 4–181, 600 North Wolfe St., Baltimore, MD 21205.

**Early Periodic Screening, Diagnosis, and Treatment Program (EPSDT).** This program screens children to identify whether health care or related services may be necessary. This federal program is available only for medicaid eligible children from birth to age twenty-one. Contact your local health department for information.

**Florida Research and Training Center.** This group offers a variety of training and consultation services for organizations interested in technical assistance with planning mental health/education services for youth. Address: 13301 North 30th Street, Tampa, FL 33612.

**Maryland State Planning Council on Developmental Disabilities.** Write to them for an excellent reader's guide that covers a national perspective on material and agencies that help parents who have children with mental, physical or emotional disabilities. Address is: 201 W. Preston St., Baltimore, MD 21202.

**Mental Health Association.** Request complimentary copies of *Fact Sheets* for preparing income tax deductions for parents of a handicapped person. Usually the state or local chapter of the MHA prepares these valuable sheets. The national office is: 1021 Prince St., Alexandria, VA 22314.

**Mental Health Law Project,** 1220 Nineteenth St., NW, Washington, DC 20036. Quarterly newsletters are available from this organization.

**Mental Health Reports.** An excellent publication that provides the reader with a concise summary of current major issues confronting people affected or associated with serving the mentally ill. Legislative areas, provider news, state issues, and special reports are provided. A resource for professionals and consumers alike. Annual subscription rate is $167. Address is: 1300 North 17th St., PO Box 9673, Arlington, VA 22209.

**National Alliance for the Mentally Ill (NAMI).** This international network comprising families of the mentally ill can provide booklists, material, and other educational information of interest to people interested in helping and advocating for the mentally ill and their families. Address is: 1901 North Fort Myer Drive, Suite 500, Arlington, VA 22209-1604.

**National Center for Clinical Infant Programs.** This group is interested in helping to ensure that comprehensive service delivery systems are planned and implemented for children from birth to age three. Address is: 733 Fifteenth St., NW, Suite 912, Washington, DC 20005.

**National Depressive and Manic Depressive Association.** Merchandise Mart, Box 3395, Chicago, IL 60654.

**National Information Center for Handicapped Children and Youth.** 1555 Wilson Boulevard, Rosslyn, VA 22209. Provides a wealth of information to parents about accessing systems that deliver services to handicapped youth.

**National Institutes of Mental Health (NIMH).** This institute was developed to address the problems associated with mental illness. Research, professional training, and providing information to the public are aims of this organization. Request from the *Public Inquiries Branch* the list of publications of the NIMH and ask to be placed on their mailing list. The lists are updated often. Ten free titles per list are allowed a person. Some excellent documents about mental illness, training, and services are available here. The National Clearinghouse for Mental Health Information is in room 15C–17. Address is: 5600 Fishers Lane, Rockville, MD 20857.

**Autism Society of America (National Society for Autistic Children and Adults).** 1234 Mass. Ave., NW, Washington, DC 20005.

**Office of Civil Rights, U.S. Department of Health and Human Services,** 330 Independence Ave. SW, Washington, DC 20201. Protection and Advocacy. These systems are set up for people of all ages who have developmental disabilities. Legal assistance may also be available.

**Parents Involved Network (PIN).** This is a self-help/advocacy group for parents of children and adolescents with emotional problems. Address is: Mental Health Assn. of Southeastern Pennsylvania, 311 South Juniper St., Philadelphia, PA 19107.

**Public Citizen Health Research Group.** This is a nonprofit organization that conducts research of interest to health consumers. The sponsored research on the *Care of the Seriously Mentally Ill: A Rating of State Programs.* (Torrey and Wolfe, authors). The report can be purchased for about $6.00. Address is: 2000 P St., NW, Washington, DC 20036.

**Rehabilitation Services Administration.** This agency is responsible for the administration of competitive discretionary grant programs totaling over $100 million. Research projects that assist disabled persons gain access to the Vocational Rehabilitation System or work are aspects of the programs they cover. The address is: Office of Developmental Programs, Room 332B, HHS Switzer Building, Third & C Streets, SW, Washington, DC 20202.

**Research and Training Center, Regional Research Institute for Human Services.** The "Families as Allies" federally funded project is located here. The purpose of the project is to develop parent/professional alliances. The staff members are conducting a much needed assessment of the needs of youths with serious emotional handicaps. *Focal Point* is their newsletter. Write and request a form, return it to the center. Such documentation of needs helps get services. Address is: Portland State University, PO Box 751, Portland, OR 97207.

**State Department of Mental Hygiene or Mental Health.** These state agencies are charged with providing public services to citizens in the respective state. Get friendly with their representatives. These are the people that you have to convince that changes are needed.

**State Department of Education.** This office can answer questions about how to get special education services in your state. Parent education programs aimed at understanding the steps in getting special services and entitlements are often conducted under the auspices of this department. They often follow up on problems implementing the regulations involved in Public Law 94–142. The *State Vocational Rehabilitation Agency is part of the State Department of Education*. Preparing handicapped persons for work is one responsibility of this agency.

**State Developmental Disabilities Agency.** This agency, assisted by the Federal Developmental Disabilities Program, has been designated to provide funding for direct services for persons with these conditions.

**State Health Department.** This agency can inform you of the health services that can be provided to your child and family.

**TAPP Project, Technical Assistance for Parent Programs,** 312 Stuart St., 2nd Floor, Boston, MA 02116. Parent training and information programs are offered.

**The Information Exchange.** This is a nonprofit corporation organized to gather and disseminate information on treating the young adult chronic patient through the use of consultation, publications, conferences, and research. The newsletter, *Tie Lines*, is very informative. Address is POB 278, Spring Valley, NY 10977.

**The Research Centers, Neuropsychiatric Institute,** UCLA, 760 Westwood Plaza, Los Angeles, Ca 90024. This is a research and training center devoted to understanding schizophrenia. Many worthwhile and informative materials are available on how to help these people adjust to community living. Much attention is devoted to behavioral approaches that help these folks.

**U.S. Department of Education, Office of Special Education and Rehabilitation Services,** Clearinghouse on the Handicapped. Washington, DC 20202. This clearinghouse provides information on federal programs and activities related to handicapped individuals. For $8.00 you can purchase the Clearinghouse's *Directory of National Information Sources on Handicapping Conditions and Related Services* which provides copious information on voluntary and consumer organizations offering services to persons with handicaps. *Programs for the Handicapped* is their newsletter.

**U.S. Department of Health and Human Services, Public Health Service,** Health Services, Rockville, MD 20857. This HSA publications may be of interest to parents who have children with physical conditions *and* emotional problems.

# REGIONAL OFFICES OF THE HEALTH CARE FINANCING ADMINISTRATION (HCFA)*

**Region 1**
Room 1309
JFK Federal Building
Boston, MA 02203

**Region 2**
Room 3811
26 Federal Plaza
New York, NY 10278

**Region 3**
3535 Market Street
P.O. Box 7760
Philadelphia, PA 19101

**Region 4**
Suite 701
101 Marietta Tower
Atlanta, GA 30323

**Region 5**
Suite A–835
175 W. Jackson Boulevard
Chicago, IL 60604

**Region 6**
Room 2000
1200 Main Tower Building
Dallas, TX 75202

**Region 7**
New Federal Office Building
Room 235
601 East 12th Street
Kansas City, MO 64106

**Region 8**
Federal Building
Room 574
1961 Stout Street
Denver, CO 80294

**Region 9**
14th Floor
100 Van Ness Avenue
San Francisco, CA 94102

**Region 10**
Mall Stop 502
2901 Third Avenue
Seattle, WA 98121

---

*To determine if a given hospital has been certified by HCFA for compliance with Medicaid regulations, contact the regional office and request the Medicare Report for Hospital X. The Freedom of Information Act allows people to have access to this information.

# Appendix D
═❋═

## OPTION 1

Jane Doe
100 Main Street
Anytown, ME.

Joint Commission on
Accreditation of Health Care Organizations (JCAH)
875 North Michigan Avenue
Chicago, Illinois 69611

Dear Sir:

I am requesting an interview with your surveyors when the JCAH survey of Hospital X occurs. Hospital X is located at the following address:

Hospital X
200 Main Street
Yourtown, Maryland 21204

My son was hospitalized on the psychiatric unit during the Fall of 1986. During that time he was placed in seclusion for 15 days with very little time out of the cell. Please examine in detail the hospitals policies on seclusion and restraints. Their use of cold wet sheet packs has often taken the form of punishment. I am basing this on the verbal reports of my son, and four other youngsters who were hospitalized on the unit. All were voluntary patients who were forced to be placed in these cold wet sheet packs. In the absence of support from well controlled scientific studies, how is it possible that such hospitals are allowed to use these old fashioned techniques? I might point out that of the many licensed psychiatric hospitals in Maryland, only two use these practices. Doesn't this also suggest a deviation from current standards of care? Please write and inform me of the date of our hearing with your representatives. You can expect to meet the parents of the four other persons who have been repeatedly wrapped up on sheets and secluded in an unreasonable manner.

Sincerely,

Jane Doe

cc Director of Psychiatry
     Hospital X

# OPTION 2

James Doe
101 Main Street
Baltimore, ME 21201


Joint Commission on Accreditation
of Health Care Organizations (JCAH)
875 North Michigan Avenue
Chicago, Illinois 60611

Dear Sir:

Please inform me of the dates of your next JCAH survey at Hospital B in Baltimore. I want to discuss some matters of concern to me about the hospital. Thank you for considering my request.

Sincerely,


James Doe

cc Director of Psychiatry
Hospital X


(The JCAH public surveys usually conduct these public information interviews on the first morning of the survey. They should not exceed two hours. A representative of the hospital will be present. In fact, the hospital staff will notify you of the location of the interview.)

## Appendix E
=❧=

# Evaluation of the Home Visit

NAME OF PERSON ON PASS _____

DATE OF VISIT _____ TIME OF VISIT_____ to _____

WARD _____

Social Worker or other professional working with the family:
_____

1. Did your child accept his prescribed medication?
   ☐ Yes    ☐ No    ☐ Somewhat
   Describe the difficulties.

2. Did your child need to be reminded about taking his
   medication?    ☐ Yes    ☐ No

3. Were there any other problems that came up about taking his
   medication?    ☐ Yes    ☐ No
   If problems occurred, what were they?

4. Did he have any eating problems?    ☐ Yes    ☐ No
   If problems occurred, what were they?

5. Did he have trouble sleeping?    ☐ Yes    ☐ No
   If problems occurred, what were they?

6. What activities was he involved with during the visit?

7. How did the activities go?     ☐ Well     ☐ Not well
   If problems occurred, please describe them.

8. Do you feel your child has benefited from this
   hospitalization?     ☐ Yes     ☐ No
   Please explain why you feel this way.

9. Was the visit satisfactory?     ☐ Yes     ☐ No
   If it was unsatisfactory, please explain what you think went
   wrong.

10. What suggestions would you like to make to the treatment
    team at this time?

11. What areas would you like help with in regard to preparing
    your relative for discharge?

12. Other comments.

Signed _____

Telephone number _____ Relationship _____

## Appendix F
===❧===

# Health Status Checklist

Read each statement very carefully before deciding if it applies to your child, then place a check mark in front of those items that describe his condition. Think in terms of, *"Does my child have difficulty with:"*

SELF CARE—requires assistance from others in regard to feeding, dressing, bathing and toileting.

☑ 1. Toileting—requires the assistance of another person.

☑ 2. Bathing—requires the help of another person.

☐ 3. Continence—difficulty in controlling either the bladder or bowels.

☐ 4. Eating—requires assistance from a person.

☐ 5. Mobility—requires the assistance of a person to walk or is confined to a wheelchair.

## COMMUNICATION

☐ 6. Speech—either lost or is so severely impaired that it can be understood only with difficulty, the person cannot carry on a normal conversation or refuses to talk.

☐ 7. Hearing—either lost or so impaired that communication problems are present.

☐  8. Vision–blind or so severely impaired that it interferes with activities of daily living.

## SPECIAL TREATMENTS REQUIRED

☐  9. Exercises–range of motion exercises or for physical enhancement.

☐ 10. Seizure precautions are necessary to consider.

☐ 11. Diabetic–checks are necessary to monitor status.

☐ 12. Other–Please specify _____

## PSYCHIATRIC CARE PROBLEMS

☑ 13. Mental status–can not understand (or remember) simple instructions, requires constant supervision for his/her own safety.

☐ 14. a. Assaultive–potential has been demonstrated on occasion in the past.

☐      b. Assaultive–currently threatening physical harm to self or others.

☐ 15. a. Suicidal risk–requires some protection and observation against impulses, low risk.

☐      b. Intermediate risk for suicide–has high potential for self injury and requires close observation.

☐      c. High risk for suicide–requires close observation and is in immediate danger of attempting suicide.

☐ 16. a. Medication required for psychiatric disorder–needs help in using these drugs.

☐      b. Medication needed for treatment–requires instruction about the drugs, side effects, toxic effects and monitoring plan.

☐ 17. Currently has hallucinations and/or delusions–requires close monitoring from staff to reduce potential jeopardy.

☐ 18. Running away–requires close observation because of potential for running away.

☐ 19. Drug Abuse.

☐ 20. Other _____

This form was adapted from the Health Status Checklist developed by Barker Bausell, Ph.D.

# Glossary

A.F.D.C.–Aid to Families with Dependent Children. It is possible to obtain cash benefits for poor families with children where one parent is absent, dead, or incapacitated.

AFFECT–How a person feels at a particular time. Anger, sadness, elation, and depression are all examples of affects. Another word for affect is mood. The type of affect, its appropriateness to the situation, and its persistence are important patterns that help determine a diagnosis. Affect can be a symptom, a sign, or a disorder.

AFFECTIVE DISORDERS–Are commonly known as mood disorders. Affective disorders influence the emotions and are cyclical. Individuals with bipolar affective disorder, known as manic depression, may suffer episodes of depression and mania alternately, with periods of normal feeling in between. The spacing between episodes varies from person to person. Unipolar affective disorder, known as severe depression, is characterized by recurrent bouts of depression without periods of mania. It is now known that persons with these disorders have differences in biochemical brain functions, which indicates in most instances the inborn nature of the disorders. Bipolar disorders have recently been linked to defective genes, thus supporting the genetic causes of some types of bipolar disorders. About 10 percent of the population suffer from these disorders. Both depression and manic-depression are *highly treatable*. Accurate diagnosis and treatment by knowledgeable professionals produce excellent results in 80 percent of the cases. The essential features of mood disorders are the same for both children and adults. DSMIIIR does not make separate categories for the two groups (see DSMIIIR later in this list).

AKATHISIA–A person who is extremely restless, may be unable to sit, and paces a lot may be described as being in a state of akathisia. Experts refer to this state as motor restlessness. It is often seen as a side effect of antipsychotic drugs.

AKINESIA–Muscle fatigue and weakness which can be inferred by less spontaneous movement of the face and body than would normally be the case. Patients may have a "zombie" like, stiff, artificial manner. May be a side effect of high potency antipsychotic drugs.

AMBIVALENCE–Holding two opposing ideas or feelings at the same time which may hinder sound decision making.

ANHEDONIA–The inability of the person to find and experience pleasure in situations or areas that were normally pleasurable or rewarding.

ANXIETY–As a mood, anxiety is a state of tension, inner unrest, apprehension, uneasiness, or a temporary psychological imbalance. The subjective feeling of anxiety may also by accompanied by physical signs such as rapid pulse, dilated pupils, heart pounding, and individual variations which may include flushed skin, irregular breathing, and cracking of the voice.

ARD COMMITTEE (ADMISSION, REVIEW AND DISMISSAL COMMIT-TEE)–This committee is made up of teachers and other professionals. It is responsible for the *admission* of handicapped children to special education, *review* of the progress of handicapped children in special education programs, and *dismissal* of handicapped children from special education.

ATTENTION–The ability to concentrate on a task.

ATTENTION DEFICIT HYPERACTIVITY DISORDER–Behavior characterized by inappropriate degrees of inattention, impulsiveness, hyperactivity. These actions appear with varying degrees in most situations affecting the child's life.

AUTISTIC–Thinking that disregards the environment in a pervasive way and constructs views of the world from internal fantasies rather than on external realities.

BLOCKING– Unexpected disruptions of one's train of thought. Some experts think the blocking occurs as a result of emotional processes.

BLOOD DYSCRASIAS–Dyscrasia refers to disease. Blood dyscrasias usually reflect the presence of abnormal cellular elements of a more-or-less permanent nature.

CATATONIA–This can be either a state of extreme agitation and overactivity referred to as *catatonic excitement* or motionless behavior often termed *catatonic negativism*. During this latter period the person may assume a strange position and rigidly hold it for long periods. This is referred to as *catatonic posturing*. Some persons resist efforts from others to move them, while other persons may resist bodily movement but end up with part of their body, such as their arms, being "molded" into peculiar positions. This process is referred to as "waxy flexibility." These reactions can be the result of a psychiatric disorder or can be related to adverse reactions to medication.

CAT SCANS–CAT refers to Computerized Axial Tomography. This type of x-ray technique makes it possible to visualize the structures of living brains. Using this painless technique, scientists can look at the brain structures and notice if abnormalities exist. Identifying brain tumors is possible. Scientists are using this technique to learn if people diagnosed with schizophrenia have enlarged brain cavities inside the brain. This information will help add another piece of information to the puzzling condition called schizophrenia.

CIRCUMSTANTIALITY–Too much digression to details and irrelevancies characterized the transactions prior to gaining the point of the conversation.

CLANGING – A form of communication in which the sound of the word, rather than its meaning, stimulates the course of later words. For example, "money, honey, funny. . ."

COMPULSIONS – The repeated, senseless performance of actions accompanied by the feeling of not being able to stop the behaviors. It is thought that these actions are performed to prevent anxiety.

COMPUTERIZED EEG – This computerized electroencephalogram is a type of brain wave test that maps electrical responses of the brain in response to different forms of stimulation.

CONCRETE THINKING – The tendency to take words literally and to attach limited meaning to language. Thinking is characteristically devoid of abstraction, hypothetical reasoning, and metaphors. Nuances of interpersonal transactions are often missed. Jokes are often misinterpreted or not understood.

CONDUCT DISORDERS – Behavioral patterns in which the basic rights of others are violated. In addition, age appropriate norms for behaving and rules are often disregarded. Aggression is common. DSMIIIR claims that the patterns must be present for at least six months.

CONFABULATION – Inventing facts which usually can't be systematically remembered to cover up impairments with thinking or performance.

CONFLICT – A clash between emotion or thoughts.

CONFUSION – A disturbance in orientation.

DELUSIONS – These are fixed, false ideas or beliefs that are made from incorrect inferences about reality. They are maintained despite evidence to the contrary.

DENIAL – Rejection of reality.

DEPERSONALIZATION – The perception that something has happened to a person's body that results in feelings of change or sensations that his body or parts of it are dead or altered.

DEPRESSION – A severe or major depression is characterized by such symptoms as: feelings of worthlessness, loss of energy and motivation, eating and sleeping disturbances, a sense of hopelessness, and recurrent thoughts of death or suicidal thoughts or attempts. Severe depression is not merely "the blues." Some types of depression may occur on a seasonal basis. The depressions are highly responsive to treatment.

DEVELOPMENTAL DISABILITY – A handicap or impairment originating before the age of eighteen which may be expected to continue indefinitely and which constitutes a substantial disability. Such conditions include pervasive developmental disorders, autism, schizophrenia, severe forms of the affective disorders and mental retardation among others.

DIAGNOSTIC AND STATISTICAL MANUAL OF MENTAL DISORDERS (DSM III-R) – The American Psychiatric Association (APA) publishes this manual which describes all of the diagnostic criteria and the systematic descriptions of the various disorders.

DISORIENTATION – The inability to accurately identify the time, place and name of the person being interviewed.

DISTRACTIBILITY – The mind is easily diverted from the conversation by unimportant detail.

DIURESIS – The production and elimination of large amounts of urine.

D.S.S. – Department of Social Services.

D.V.R. – Department of Vocational Services.

DYSTONIA – Acute muscular spasms, often of the tongue, jaw, eyes, neck, and sometimes of the entire body. These can be associated with the use of some psychoactive medications and can be alleviated with medication prescribed to counteract the symptoms.

ECHOLALIA – The persistent repetition of words.

ECHOPRAXIA – Mimicking another person's movements.

ECT-Electroconvulsive therapy used in the treatment of some types of depression among adults.

EDUCATION FOR ALL HANDICAPPED CHILDREN ACT – The federal law that guarantees all handicapped children the right to a free appropriate public education. It is Public Law 94–142.

EUPHORIA – Exaggerated sense of well being.

EXTRAPYRAMIDAL SYNDROME – A variety of signs and symptoms, including muscular rigidity, tremors, drooling, shuffling gait (parkinsonism); restlessness (akathesia); peculiar involuntary postures (dystonias); motor inertia (akinesia), and many other neurological disorders.

FANTASY – Imagined thoughts to gratify wishes.

FLIGHT OF IDEAS–Thoughts and speech that occur in rapid succession and may be incoherent.

FRUSTRATION–An interference with a goal.

G.P.A.–General Public Assistance.

GUILT–A distressing emotion that is felt when someone has violated his values; such a person may feel worthless and seek punishment.

GRANDIOSITY–Unrealistic feelings of great importance, exaggerated euphoria and delusions of grandeur. An example is, "I am God."

HALLUCINATION–The perception of a sensory stimulus in the absence of such a stimulus. These false perceptions in the senses (hearing, seeing, tasting, smell ing and touching) are not based on reality. The person experiencing these sensations believes that they are real. Sometimes they may act on the basis of the false perceptions of reality.
  (a) Auditory hallucinations indicate that a person is hearing sounds that are not there.
  (b) Visual hallucinations are false perceptions of sight.
  (c) Olfactory hallucinations mean that a person smells odors that are not present.
  (d) Gustatory hallucinations refer to invalid perceptions of taste.
  (e) Tactile hallucinations refer to invalid perceptions of touch. Such a person may perceive that something is crawling on his skin.
  (f) Somatic hallucinations may take the form of falsely perceiving that something is happening to one's body.

HYPERACTIVITY–Excessive activity which is generally purposeful.

HYPERKINETIC SYNDROME–This disorder is now referred to as Attention Deficit Hyperactivity Disorder (ADHD). Such persons often are inattentive, impulsive, and hyperactive in comparison to persons of similar ages.

HYPOMANIA–Excitement that is "greater than average" but less than a full blown, disorganized manic episode. People have described the mood as a "nice high."

IATROGENIC– Distress or illness created by a physician.

IDEAS OF REFERENCE–This occurs when a patient feels that special events, such as television broadcasts, have special reference to him.

IEP–Individualized Education Program. The written plan that describes what services the local education agency has promised to provide to your child.

ILLUSIONS–Misperceptions of real sensory stimuli.

INFORMED CONSENT – Permission for treatment based on an understanding of the purpose of treatment, common side effects or risks, consequences of withholding treatment permission, approximate length of treatment, and alternative treatment modalities.

IRP – Individualized Rehabilitation Plan.

IRRITABILITY – An inner feeling or tension or disequilibrium often communicated to others as annoyance, anger, or frustration.

ITP – Individualized Treatment Plan. This multidisciplinary plan of treatment must be written in the medical record, which is a legal document.

LABILE – Unstable emotions.

LEA (LOCAL EDUCATION AGENCY) – The county school system responsible for educating your child.

LOOSENESS OF ASSOCIATION – Speech in which ideas have no relation to each other.

MAGICAL THINKING – Speech that reveals that a person's thinking indicates that his actions and/or thoughts will result in outcomes that defy logic.

MANIA – A mood characterized by such symptoms as – rapid or unpredictable emotional changes, high energy level, feelings of grandiosity, extreme irritability, and excessive involvement in activities that have high potential for painful consequences which are not recognized during the manic period.

MEDICAID – A government program which pays medical costs for low income people. Recipients of SSI, GPA, AFDC, and PAA are automatically covered by Medicaid in most states. Other low income people may also be eligible for these benefits.

MEDICARE – Health insurance for people sixty-five or older and for persons who have been entitled to SSDI for two years or longer.

MENTAL RETARDATION – Below average general intellectual functioning which coexists with deficits in adaptive behavior.

MOOD – Pervasive feeling states that are experienced subjectively.

MRI – This refers to Magnetic Resonance Imaging, a technique involving exact measurements of brain structures based on the effects of a magnetic field on various substances in the brain. Occasionally this technique is referred to as nuclear magnetic resonance (NMR).

MUTISM – Not speaking.

NEOLOGISMS – Using words in a distorted manner, creating new words, or giving special meaning to standard words.

NEUROLEPTIC – Medicines which produce symptoms resembling those diseases of the nervous system.

NEUROLEPTIC MALIGNANT SYNDROME – This is a life threatening complication, usually due to administration of neuroleptic drugs. Elevated temperature combined with muscular rigidity are common features of this disorder. Excessive perspiration, high blood pressure, rapid pulse rate, and changes in the level of consciousness also occur. Once begun, symptoms rapidly progress. Mortality rates range from 20 to 30 percent.

OBSESSIONS – Ideas or thoughts that persistently intrude into consciousness.

ORGANIC – Disorders in which psychological or behavioral abnormalities are associated with transient or permanent dysfunction of the brain.

P.A.A. – Public Assistance to Adults.

PANIC ATTACKS – Sudden, irrational bouts of anxiety which can produce extreme distress, feelings of doom, and panic. The attacks are accompanied by the physiological signs of anxiety.

PARANOIA – A mental disorder featuring delusions of persecution and suspiciousness. Often the person also has delusions of grandeur and may feel that "the world is out to get him."

PARKINSONISM – A neurological disorder characterized by a rapid, coarse tremor, pill-rolling movements, masklike faces, cogwheel rigidity, drooling, akinesia, slowness in movement, or gait disturbance.

PUBLIC LAW 94–142 – This act refers to the Education for All Handicapped Children Act. It mandated public educational systems to provide educational service to *all* handicapped children in the least restrictive environment.

PERSONALITY DISORDER – Persistent, characteristic, maladaptive ways of behaving.

PET SCANS – PET stands for Positron Emission Tomography. This procedure allows for a way to measure the metabolic activity of specific areas of the brain, even areas that are located deep in the brain. This technique then provides information about the function of the brain. It is providing useful information about the living brain and adding to our knowledge about the major mental illnesses.

"PILL ROLLING"–Rhythmic rubbing of the index finger and the thumb.

PHOBIA–Unrealistic and irrational anxiety that is felt for an object or place.

PHOTOSENSITIVITY–Increased sensitivity of the skin to the sun leading to sun-burning more easily than usual. Some psychoactive medications increase this likelihood.

PRESERVATION–Repetitive movement or speech that is thought to be created by the person's own inner preoccupations. Such behavior occurs frequently among persons with organic illnesses.

PSYCHOTROPIC DRUG–A drug that has an effect on psychic function, behavior, or experience.

PSYCHOSIS–This term usually means that a person is out of touch with reality and cannot distinguish fact from fantasy.

RCBF–Refers to Regional Cerebral Blood Flow. The procedure calls for a person to inhale a radioactive gas and the rate of disappearance of this substance from different areas of the brain provides information about the activity of brain regions during various mental activities.

REALITY TESTING–The ability to accurately distinguish fact from fantasy. To make sense of one's environment.

SCHIZOPHRENIA–A major psychiatric disorder, probably with multiple causes, characterized by disturbances in content and form of thought, perception, affect, sense of self, volition, relationship to the external world, and psychomotor behavior.

SEA–The State Education Agency.

S.G.A.– Substantial Gainful Activity. This term has reference to obtaining entitlements.

S.S.D.I.–Social Security Disability Insurance. This money has been paid into the Social Security system through payroll deductions on earnings. Disabled workers are entitled to such benefits. People who become disabled prior to the age of twenty-two may collect SSDI under a parent's account, if the parent is retired, disabled, or deceased.

S.S.I.–Supplemental Security Income is available for low income persons who are disabled, blind, or aged. SSI is based on need, not on past earnings.

STEREOTYPY–Purposeless movements which are repetitive and odd.

TANGENTIALITY – A disturbance in interpersonal communication characterized by the person bringing up a point, getting off the track, and never making the original point.

TARDIVE DYSKINESIA – Involuntary movements of the mouth, tongue, and lips can occur and may be associated with choreo-atheroid (purposeless, quick, jerky movements that occur suddenly) movements of the trunk and limbs. Psychotropic medication contributes to the development of this condition.

VEGETATIVE SIGNS – These are the biological signs of depression. They are insomnia, anorexia, weight loss, diurnal (day/night) mood variation, constipation, and diminished libido.

# Reading List

The Reading List is divided into each chapter of the book. There are two lists; one general reading and the other more technical but still easily understood books. This is not a complete list but will serve to introduce you to other worthwhile books on the subject. The Reading List at the end of each chapter is a listing of references used by the author of each chapter and is another fine source of further readings.

## Chapter 1

Andreasen, Nancy. *The Broken Brain: The Biological Revolution in Psychiatry.* New York: Harper and Row, 1984.

Arieti, Silvano. *Understanding and Helping the Schizophrenic: A Guide for Family and Friends.* New York: Simon and Schuster, 1981.

Bernheim, Kayla. *Schizophrenia: Symptoms, Causes, Treatments.* New York: Norton, 1979.

Bohn, John and James W. Jefferson. *Lithium and Manic Depression: A Guide.* Madison: University of Wisconsin. (Lithium Information Center. 600 Highland Ave., Madison, WI 53729), 1982.

Cantor, Sheila. *The Schizophrenic Child: A Primer for Parents and Professionals.* The Eden Press, 1982; distributed by University of Toronto Press.

Fieve, Ronald. *Moodswing: The Third Revolution in Psychiatry.* New York: Bantam Books, 1976.

Garson, Sascha. *Out of our Minds.* New York: Prometheus Books, 1986.

Gattozzi, Ruth. *What's Wrong with My Child?* New York: McGraw-Hill, 1986.

Kline, Nathan. *From Sad to Glad.* New York: Random House, 1981.

Knitzer, Jane. *Unclaimed Children.* Washington, D.C.: Children's Defense Fund (122 C St., NW, Washington, D.C. 20001), 1982.

Lickey, Marvin and Barbara Gordon. *Drugs for Mental Illness — A Revolution in Psychiatry.* New York: W. H. Freeman, 1983.

Medenwald, Janet R., John H. Greist, and James W. Jefferson. *Carbamazepine and Manic Depression: A Guide*. Madison: University of Wisconsin (Dept. of Psychiatry, Center for Health Services, Lithium Information Center. 600 Highland Ave., Madison, WI 53729), 1987.

Oishi, Sabine and Jeanne Simons. *The Hidden Child: The Linwood Method for Reaching the Autistic Child*. Kensington, MD: Woodbine House, 1986.

Park, Clara and Leon Shapiro. *You Are Not Alone: Understanding and Dealing with Mental Illness*. Boston: Little, Brown, 1976.

Sheehan, Susan. *Is There No Place on Earth for Me?* New York, Random House, 1983.

Torrey, E. Fuller. *Surviving Schizophrenia: A Family Manual*. New York: Harper and Row, 1983.

Walsh, Maryellen. *Schizophrenia: Straight Talk for Families and Friends*. New York: Wm. Morrow, 1985.

Wender, Paul. *Mind, Mood and Medicine: A Guide to the New Biopsychiatry*. New York: Meridian Books, 1981.

## Chapter 2

Binkard, Betty, Marge Goldberg, and Paula F. Goldberg. *A Guidebook for Parents of Children with Emotional Disorders*. Minneapolis, MN: Pacer Center, Inc. (4826 Chicago Ave., Minneapolis, MN 55417), 1984.

Dickman, Irving R. and Sol Gordon. *Getting Help for a Disabled Child: Advice from Parents*. New York: Public Affairs Pamphlet (Public Affairs Committee, Inc., 381 Park Ave. South, New York, NY 10016), 1983.

Hinckley, Jack and Jo Ann Hinckley. *Breaking Points*. New York: Berkley Publishing Corp., 1985.

Kanter, Joel. *Coping Strategies for Relatives of the Mentally Ill*. Arlington: National Alliance for the Mentally Ill, 1984.

Vine, Phyllis. *Families in Pain: Children, Siblings, Spouses, and Parents Speak Out*. Westminster, MD: Pantheon Press, 1982.

## Chapter 3

Korpell, Herbert. *How You Can Help . . . A Guide for Families of Psychiatric Hospital Patients*. Washington, D.C.: American Psychiatric Press, 1984.

# Chapter 4

Featherstone, Helen. *A Difference in the Family: Living with a Disabled Child*. New York: Penguin Books, 1981.

Towne, Sally, Joyce R. Borden, and Cheryl Cutrona. *Philadelphia Community Access for Children and Adolescents: A Book for Parents and Professionals*. Philadelphia: Mental Health Assn. of Southeastern Pennsylvania, 1986.

# Chapter 5

Colley, Relan. "The Education for All Handicapped Children Act: A Statutory and Legal Analysis." *Journal of Law and Education* 10 (1981): 137–61. An excellent review of the provisions of the act and the protection provided to parents and adults.

*A Guidebook for Parents of Children with Emotional Disorders*. Minneapolis: PACER Center (Parent Advocacy Coalition for Educational Rights 4826 Chicago Avenue South, Minneapolis, MN 55417, (612) 827–2916). This is an excellent information book for parents of mentally ill children. It focuses on resources in the state of Minnesota but also provides information of general relevance in any state.

*Handicapped Students and Special Education*. Rosemount, MN: Data Research Inc.(P.O. Box 405, Rosemount, Minnesota 55068), 1985. This source contains the text of the EHC and synopses of relevant case law.

Russell, L. Mark. *Alternatives: A Family Guide to Legal and Financial Planning for the Disabled*. Evanston, IL: First Publications, 1983.

Yohalem, Daniel and Janet Dinsmore. *94–142 and 504: Numbers that Add Up to Educational Rights for Handicapped Children: A Guide for Parents and Advocates*. Washington, D.C.: Children's Defense Fund (122 C St., NW, Washington, D.C. 20001), 1984.

# Chapter 6

Apter, Steven J. and Jane Close Conoley. *Childhood Behavior Disorders and Emotional Disturbances*. Englewood Cliffs, NJ: Prentice-Hall, 1984.

Apter, Steven J. *Troubled Children: Troubled Systems*. New York: Pergamon Press, 1982.

Egeland, J. A., D.S. Gerhard, D. L. Pauls, J. N. Sussex, K.K. Kid, R. A. Cleona, A. M. Hestter, and Houseman. "Bipolar Affective Disorders Linked to DNA markers on Chromosome 11." *Nature* 325, no. 26 (February, 1987): 783–87.

Fass, Larry A. *The Emotionally Disturbed Child.* Springfield, IL: Chas. C. Thomas, 1975.

McDowell, Richard L., Gary W. Adamson, and Frank H. Wood. *Teaching Emotionally Disturbed Children.* Boston: Little, Brown and Company, 1982.

Reinert, Henry R. *Children in Conflict.* 2d ed. St. Louis: The C.V. Mosby Company, 1980.

# Chapter 7

Giovacchini, Peter. *The Urge to Die: Why Young People Commit Suicide.* Macmillan: New York, 1981.

Gold, Mark S. *The Good News about Depression: Cures and Treatments in the New Age of Psychiatry.* New York: Villard Books, 1986.

Greist, John and James Jefferson. *Depression and Its Treatment: Help for the Nation's #1 Mental Problem.* Washington, D.C.: American Psychiatric Press, 1984.

Hafen, Brent Q. and Kathryn J. Frandsen. *Youth Suicide: Depression and Loneliness.* Evergreen, CO: Cordillera Press, 1986.

McCoy, Kathleen. *Coping with Teenage Depression: A Parent's Guide.* New York: New American Library, 1982.

McKnew, Donald, Leon Cytryn, and Herbert Yahraes. *Why Isn't Johnny Crying? Coping with Depression in Children.* New York: W.W. Norton & Co., 1983.

Papolos, Demitri, F. and Janice Papolos. *Overcoming Depression.* New York: Harper and Row, 1987.

Rosenfeld, Linda and Marilynne Prupas. *Left Alive.* Charles C. Thomas: Springfield, IL, 1984.

# Chapter 8

Hatfield, Agnes. *Coping with Mental Illness in the Family: A Family Guide.* National Alliance for the Mentally Ill, 1984.

Hatfield, Agnes and Harriet P. Lefley, eds. *Families of the Mentally Ill: Coping and Adaptation.* New York: Guilford Press, 1987.

Hyde, Alexander. *Living with Schizophrenia.* Chicago: Contemporary Books, 1980.

Morrison, James. *Your Brother's Keeper: A Guide for Families of the Mentally Ill.* Chicago: Nelson-Hall, 1981.

Oliver, B. *The ABC's of Hanging on While Raising a Family with a Disturbed Child.* Westwego, LA: Flo-Bet Press, 1976.

Turnbull, Ann P. and H. Turnbull. *Parents Speak Out: Views from the Other Side of the 2 Way Mirror.* Columbus, OH: Chas. E. Merrill, 1978.

Wasow, Mona. *Coping with Schizophrenia: A Survival Manual for Parents, Relatives, and Friends.* Palo Alto, CA: Science & Behavior Books, 1982.

# Technical But Readable Books

## Chapter 1

American Psychiatric Association. *Diagnostic and Statistical Manual of Mental Disorders,* 3d. ed., rev. Washington, D.C.:American Psychiatric Assn. Press, 1987. This 567 page manual can be purchased for $29.95 plus postage by writing to: American Psychiatric Press, Inc.,
Order Dept.
1400 K Street, N.W., 11th Floor
Washington, D.C. 20005;

American Psychiatric Association. *Psychiatric Glossary.* Washington, D.C.: American Psychiatric Assn. Press, 1984.

Biederman, Joseph and Michael Jellimek. "Current Concepts: Psychopharmacology in Children." *The New England Journal of Medicine* 310, no. 15 (April, 12, 1984): 968–72.

Brim, Orville G. and Jerome Kagan, eds. *Constancy and Change in Human Development.* Cambridge: Harvard University Press, 1980.

Cantwell, Dennis P. and Gabrielle A. Carlson. *Affective Disorders in Childhood and Adolescence: An Update.* New York: SP Medical & Scientific Books, 1983.

Chess, Stella and Alexander Thomas. *Temperament in Clinical Practice.* New York: Guilford Press, 1986.

Eysenck, Hans. *Decline and Fall of the Freudian Empire.* New York: Viking Penguin, 1985.

Franklin, Jon. *Molecules of the Mind.* New York: Atheneum, 1987.

Gottsman, Irving I. *Schizophrenia and Genetic Risks*. Arlington: National Alliance for the Mentally Ill (1901 N. Ft. Myer Dr., #500, Arlington, VA 22209), 1984.

Kaufman, J.M. *Characteristics of Children's Behavior Disorders*. Columbus, OH: Chas. E. Merrill, 1981.

Maxmen, Jerrold S. *Essential Psychopathology*. New York: W.W. Norton & Co., 1986.

Maxmen, Jerrold S. *The New Psychiatry: How Modern Psychiatrists Think about Their Patients, Theories, Diagnoses, Drugs, Psychotherapies, Power, Training, Families and Private Lives*. New York: Wm. Morrow and Co., 1985.

Mussen, Paul Henry et al. *Child Development and Personality*. 6th ed. New York: Harper and Row, 1984.

Rutter, Michael and Henri Giller. *Juvenile Delinquency: Trends and Perspectives*. New York: Guilford Press, 1984.

Twiford, Rainer. *A Child with a Problem: A Guide to Psychological Disorders of Children*. Englewood Cliffs, NJ: Prentice-Hall, 1979.

# Chapter 2

Goldstein, Joseph, Anna Freud, and Albert J. Solnit. *Beyond the Best Interests of the Child*. New York: Free Press, 1973.

# Chapter 5

Goldberg, Steven S. *Special Education Law: A Guide for Parents, Advocates and Educators*. New York: Plenum Press, 1982.

Jones, Philip R. *A Practical Guide to Federal Special Education Law: Understanding and Implementing PL 94–142*. New York: Holt, Rinehart & Winston, 1981.

Morse, W.C. et al. *Affective Education for Special Children and Youth*. Reston, VA: Council for Exceptional Children (1920 Association Dr., Reston, VA 22091), 1980.

Reinert, H.C. *Children in Conflict*. St. Louis: C.V. Mosby, 1980.

# Chapter 6

Apter, Steven J. and Jane Close Conoley. *Childhood Behavior Disorders and Emotional Disturbances: An Introduction to Teaching Troubled Children*. Englewood Cliffs, NJ: Prentice-Hall, 1984.

Algozzine, R., R. Schmid, and C.D. Mercer. *Childhood Behavior Disorders: Applied Research and Educational Practice*. Rockville, MD: Aspens Systems Corp., 1981.

Blakenship, C. and S.A. Lilly. *Mainstreaming Students with Learning Behavior Problems*. New York: Holt, Rinehart & Winston, 1981.

Stainback, S. and W. Stainbeck. *Educating Children with Severe Maladaptive Behaviors*. New York: Grune and Stratton, 1980.

# Chapter 7

Peck, Michael et al., eds. *Youth Suicide*. New York: Springer, 1985.

Rutter, Michael et al., eds. *Depression in Young People*. New York: Guilford Press, 1985.

# Chapter 8

Association for Retarded Citizens. *How to Provide for Their Future*. Arlington, TX: Association for Retarded Citizens (National Headquarters, PO Box 6109, Arlington, TX 76011), 1984.

Hatfield, Agnes B. *Consumer Guide to Mental Health Services*. Arlington, VA: National Alliance for the Mentally Ill, 1985

Russell, Mark. *Alternatives: A Family Guide to Legal and Financial Planning for the Disabled*. Evanston: First Publications, 1983. Available from National Alliance for the Mentally Ill, 1901 N. Fort Myer Drive, #500, Arlington, VA 22209.

Stroul, Beth. *Models of Community Support Services: Approaches to Helping Persons With Long Term Mental Illness*. National Institute of Mental Health Community Support Program, August, 1986. Available from Center for Psychiatric Rehabilitation, Sargent College of Allied Health Professions, Boston University, 1019 Commonwealth Ave., Boston, MA 02215.

Torrey, E. Fuller and Sidney M. Wolfe. *Care of the Seriously Mentally Ill: A Rating of State Programs*. Washington, D.C.: Public Citizen Health Research Group (200 P St., NW, Washington, D.C. 20036), 1986.

Torrey, E. Fuller, M.D. *Surviving Schizophrenia: A Family Manual*. New York: Harper and Row, 1983.

U.S. Department of Education. *Pocket Guide to Federal help for the Disabled Person* (Publication No. E–85–22002), February, 1985. Can be ordered from Office of Information and Resources for the Handicapped, Washington, DC 20202.

# Index

## About the Authors

Dr. Alp Karahasan is not only a board certified child psychiatrist, but also possesses a doctorate in biochemistry. Such credentials, in the light of the emphasis on brain research and the new age of psychiatry, make his contributions especially important. Dr. Karahasan has conducted research and taught in the Division of Child Psychiatry at the University of Maryland, among other universities. Until recently, he was the Director of Mental Hygiene in Maryland, where he mandated the development of the "Five Year Plan" for the public psychiatric sector and started work on the "Five Year Plan for Children and Adolescent Services" that was later developed by the organization.

Dr. Paul McElroy, parent and educator, is a graduate of Johns Hopkins University. He was the first president of the Alliance for the Mentally Ill of Maryland. He teaches courses in school law, administration, and educational policy at Morgan State University and Johns Hopkins University.

Terry Rosenberg is one of the founders of the Alliance for the Mentally Ill chapter that serves children, adolescents, and their families.

Carol Howe is the mother of two sons with schizophrenia. Her master's degree is in early special childhood education. She is nationally known as a speaker and advocate of services and information for the families of the mentally ill.

# The Special Needs Collection

Woodbine House is pleased to offer these fine books for parents of children with special needs and the professionals who assist them.

**CHILDREN AND ADOLESCENTS WITH MENTAL ILLNESS: A Parents Guide**
*Edited by Evelyn McElroy, Ph.D. Woodbine House, 1987. 235p. charts. graphs. index. resource guide. reading list. glossary. appendices. paperback (0-933149-10-7).*

**CHILDREN WITH EPILEPSY: A Parents Guide**
*Edited by Helen Reisner. Woodbine House, 1987. 230p. charts. graphs. photographs. index. glossary. resource guide. reading list. illus. paperback (0-933149-19-0).*

**CHOICES IN DEAFNESS: A Parents Guide**
*Edited by Sue Schwartz, Ph.D. Woodbine House, 1987. 212p. charts. graphs. illus. resource guide. reading list. index. paperback (0-933142-09-3).*

**LANGUAGE OF TOYS: Teaching Communication Skills to Special Needs Children: A Parents Guide**
*By Sue Schwartz and Joan E. Heller Miller. Woodbine House, 1987. 160p. charts. graphs. photographs. illustrations. glossary. resource guide. reading list. paperback (0-933149-08-5).*

**THE HIDDEN CHILD: The Linwood Method for Reaching the Autistic Child**
*By Jeanne Simons and Sabine Oishi, Ph.D. Woodbine House, 1987. 250p. illus. index. bibliography. paperback (0-933142-06-9).*

**BABIES WITH DOWN SYNDROME: A New Parents Guide**
*Edited by Karen Stray-Gundersen. Woodbine House, 1986. 237p. charts. graphs. index. resource guide. reading list. illus. paperback (0-933149-02-6).*

| | Quantity | Price | Total |
|---|---|---|---|
| *Children and Adolescents with Mental Illness* | | $12.95 | |
| *Children with Epilepsy* | | $12.95 | |
| *Choices in Deafness* | | $12.95 | |
| *Language of Toys* | | $ 9.95 | |
| *The Hidden Child* | | $17.95 | |
| *Babies with Down Syndrome* | | $ 9.95 | |
| | | Subtotal | |
| | Shipping/Handling ($1.50 per copy) | | |
| | Tax (5% for MD residents only) | | |
| | | **TOTAL** | |

**SHIP TO:**

NAME _____

ADRESS _____

_____

_____ ZIP _____

TELEPHONE _____

VISA/MasterCard # _____ EXP. DATE _____

Return Order Form to: Woodbine House, 10400 Connecticut Avenue, Kensington, MD 20895. Or **Order Toll Free 800-843-7323** (outside Maryland), 301-949-3590 (in Maryland). Also available in fine bookstores.
**Thank you for your order.**